P9-CNI-922

# Better Homes and Gardens

# ENCYCLOPEDIA
## of
# COOKING

*Volume 4*

Cook a head of cauliflower whole and let the creamy white head be a showpiece on the vegetable platter. Or, leave it uncooked and use flowerets in vegetable salads for a special touch.

**On the cover:** Easy, yet elegant, best describes Cherries Jubilee. After the lights have been dimmed, the sauce is flamed at the table with brandy, then spooned over ice cream.

## BETTER HOMES AND GARDENS BOOKS
### NEW YORK • DES MOINES

©Meredith Corporation, 1970. All Rights Reserved.
Printed in the United States of America.
Second Printing, 1970.
Library of Congress Catalog Card Number: 73-129265
SBN 696-02004-1

**CAULIFLOWER**—A vegetable of the cabbage family having a compact, creamy white head, called a curd. Made up of tight clusters of flower buds, the curd is ready for eating before these buds open. The curd is surrounded with large green leaves. The outer leaves are often pinned or tied over the curd to help keep out foreign materials and to bleach or whiten the head as it matures. Although the curd is the part usually eaten, the leaves and stems can also be cooked and used in soups.

The name cauliflower comes from the Latin words *caulis* meaning stem, stalk, or cabbage, and *floris* meaning flower. Cauliflower has been used for many centuries—the earliest date around the sixth century B.C. in the Mediterranean area. The Italians have cultivated this vegetable since the 1500's. Through the years they have developed several cauliflower varieties including small green- or purple-headed types different from the common white-headed vegetable found in grocery stores.

Cauliflower became popular throughout Europe and eventually was brought to America. For about 200 years it was grown in this country almost exclusively by Italian families in New England. Since the 1920's, however, cauliflower has been grown widely in the United States; California, New York, Oregon, and Washington are the main producers. Because cauliflower thrives in moist climates with warm days and cool nights, the majority of the cauliflower crop comes from California.

*Nutritional value:* Here is an excellent source of vitamin C, especially when eaten raw: one cup of uncooked cauliflower meets the day's requirements for an adult. For those counting calories cauliflower is a must. One cup of cauliflower, raw or cooked, contains about 25 calories.

*How to select:* Overall appearance is the most helpful quality indicator for selecting cauliflower. Look for a head of cauliflower that is clean, heavy, and compact. It should have white or creamy white flowerets and a bright green jacket of leaves. Head size does not affect the quality, and leaves that sometimes grow through the curd may be ignored.

Avoid a cauliflower head that has many brown bruises, a speckled appearance, or if its leaves are yellowed or withered. Also avoid cauliflower that is beginning to break apart. These are all indications that the head has "passed its prime."

The peak season for cauliflower is from September through November. It can, however, be found in markets throughout the year. As purchased in the supermarket, it usually has most of its jacket leaves removed and often is covered in a clear wrapper. You can plan on four to six servings from a head of cauliflower that weighs 2½ to 3 pounds. Frozen cauliflower with or without a cheese sauce can be purchased year-round.

*How to store:* Keep fresh cauliflower refrigerated. To retard the wilting of green leaves, sprinkle with water then cover the head tightly in foil, clear plastic wrap, or place in a covered container.

To freeze, wash it thoroughly and cut into flowerets or pieces one inch thick. Blanch in boiling water for three minutes. Then chill in ice water three minutes and drain well. Pack tightly in moisture-vapor-proof containers. Seal, label with contents and date, then freeze. Generally, 1⅓ pounds cleaned and trimmed cauliflower yields about one pint when frozen.

*How to prepare:* Cauliflower may be cooked whole or broken first into flowerets. Or, simply wash and eat—uncooked.

To prepare, remove leaves and some of the woody stem. Cook, covered, in a small amount of boiling salted water until the cauliflower is just tender when tested with a fork. Generally, the whole head will cook in 20 to 25 minutes and flowerets in 10 to 15 minutes. Overcooking, even for only a few minutes, causes the vegetable to turn dark and the flavor to become strong and unpleasant, so test frequently.

*How to use:* This is a truly versatile and delicious vegetable. For example, include raw cauliflower flowerets as vegetable dippers on a platter of appetizers. Cauliflower and well-seasoned sour cream or cream cheese dips make excellent companions on your hors d'oeuvre tray.

Cauliflower makes a delicious addition to salads and adds an unusual crispness. Some flowerets are cooked while others are added to the salad uncooked.

## Cauliflower-Ham Salad

    1 medium head cauliflower, broken into flowerets
    2 cups fully-cooked ham cut in strips
    ½ cup thin radish slices
    ½ cup sliced celery
    ½ cup mayonnaise or salad dressing
    2 tablespoons milk
    1 teaspoon sugar
    2 teaspoons prepared horseradish
    Lettuce cups

In a saucepan cook flowerets, covered, in a small amount of boiling salted water for 10 to 15 minutes; drain thoroughly. Toss with ham, radish slices, and celery; chill.

For dressing stir together mayonnaise or salad dressing, milk, sugar, and horseradish. Spoon cauliflower-ham mixture into lettuce cups and serve with dressing. Makes 6 servings.

## Cauliflower Vinaigrette

    1 medium head cauliflower, broken into flowerets
    ⅔ cup salad oil
    ¼ cup white wine vinegar
    1 large tomato, chopped
    ⅓ cup chopped pimiento-stuffed green olives
    2 tablespoons chopped green onion
    1 tablespoon pickle relish
    1 teaspoon salt
    1 teaspoon paprika
    ⅛ teaspoon pepper

Cook flowerets, covered, in small amount of boiling salted water till just crisp-tender, about 10 minutes. Drain; place in shallow dish.

Combine oil, vinegar, tomato, olives, onion, relish, salt, paprika, and pepper. Pour over cauliflower; chill 2 to 3 hours. At serving time drain off excess oil and vinegar. Serve in lettuce-lined bowl and garnish with tomato wedges, if desired. Makes 8 to 10 servings.

## Tangy Cauliflower Salad

    1 medium head cauliflower, broken into flowerets (about 4 cups)
    2 medium carrots, cut in julienne strips (1 cup)
    ⅓ cup French salad dressing
    • • •
    ½ ounce blue cheese, crumbled (2 tablespoons)
    Lettuce cups
    1 small avocado, peeled and sliced

Cut flowerets in half lengthwise. Combine cauliflower and carrot strips; toss with French dressing. Cover and refrigerate till ready to serve, stirring once or twice.

At serving time, sprinkle with blue cheese. Toss lightly and serve in crisp lettuce cups. Top each serving with avocado slices. Serves 6.

Cheese and cauliflower are natural go-togethers. A hot soup made with cheese, cauliflower, and broth is a gourmet's delight. Serve it as a main dish or as an appetizer soup.

## Creamy Cauliflower Soup

    1 medium head cauliflower, broken into flowerets
    ¼ cup chopped onion
    ¼ cup butter or margarine
    ¼ cup all-purpose flour
    3 cups chicken broth
    2 cups milk
    1 teaspoon Worcestershire sauce
    4 ounces sharp process American cheese, shredded (1 cup)
    Snipped chives

Cook flowerets, covered, in small amount of boiling salted water till tender, 10 to 15 minutes; drain and coarsely chop.

In large saucepan cook onion in butter till tender but not brown. Blend in flour. Add chicken broth, milk, and Worcestershire sauce. Cook and stir till mixture thickens slightly. Add cauliflower. Bring to boiling and stir in cheese. Sprinkle each serving with snipped chives. Makes 6 to 8 servings.

## Summary Scramble

Summer Scramble

    2 tablespoons butter or margarine
  ½ cup chopped onion
    1 small clove garlic, crushed
  ¼ cup snipped parsley
    1 teaspoon salt
    1 teaspoon seasoned salt
      Dash pepper
      Dash dried thyme leaves,
        crushed
    1 medium head cauliflower, broken
        into small flowerets
    3 large tomatoes, diced
    2 small zucchini, sliced

In a large saucepan melt butter or margarine; cook onion and garlic until tender but not brown. Add remaining ingredients. Cover tightly. Simmer 15 to 20 minutes; uncover and cook about 10 minutes longer. Serve in sauce dishes with juice. Makes 10 servings.

For a change of pace prepare cauliflower for the vegetable course at your next meal. Here's a simple vegetable accompaniment: top cooked cauliflower with melted butter, then dash very lightly with nutmeg. Or, drizzle browned butter atop cooked cauliflower. (See also *Vegetable*.)

Crisp-cooked cauliflower marinates in a tangy salad dressing several hours before Cauliflower Vinaigrette is ready to serve. Plump tomato wedges arranged on top add a perky note.

## Cheese Frosted Cauliflower

1 medium head cauliflower
  Salt
½ cup mayonnaise or salad
  dressing
2 teaspoons prepared mustard
3 ounces sharp process American
  cheese, shredded (¾ cup)

Remove leaves and trim base from cauliflower. Wash. Cook whole, covered, in boiling salted water for 12 to 15 minutes. Drain. Place in *ungreased* shallow baking pan. Sprinkle with salt.

Combine mayonnaise and mustard; spread over cauliflower. Top with cheese. Bake at 375° till cheese is melted and bubbly, about 10 minutes. Makes 4 or 5 servings.

## Cauliflower and Dilly Shrimp

1 medium head cauliflower
    • • •
2 tablespoons butter or margarine
2 tablespoons all-purpose flour
½ teaspoon dried dillweed
¼ teaspoon salt
  Dash pepper
1¼ cups milk
1 cup cleaned cooked shrimp,
  cut up

Cook whole cauliflower, covered, in small amount of boiling salted water till tender, about 15 to 20 minutes; drain well.

Meanwhile in a small saucepan melt butter over low heat. Blend in flour, dillweed, salt, and pepper. Add milk all at once. Cook and stir till thickened and bubbly. Add shrimp; heat through. Place hot cauliflower on serving plate. Drizzle with a little shrimp sauce. Pass remaining sauce. Makes 4 servings.

## Company Cauliflower

1 medium head cauliflower, broken
  into flowerets
  Salt and pepper
1 cup dairy sour cream
4 ounces sharp process American
  cheese, shredded (1 cup)
2 teaspoons sesame seed, toasted

Cook flowerets, covered, in small amount of boiling salted water till tender, 10 to 15 minutes; drain well. Place *half* the flowerets in a 1-quart casserole. Season with salt and pepper. Spread with *half* the sour cream and *half* the cheese. Top with 1 teaspoon sesame seed. Repeat layers with remaining ingredients.

Bake casserole at 350° till the shredded cheese melts and sour cream is heated through, about 5 minutes. Makes 6 servings.

## Cauliflower Scallop

1 10½-ounce can condensed cream
  of celery soup
2 beaten eggs
2 ounces sharp Cheddar cheese,
  shredded (½ cup)
½ cup soft bread crumbs
¼ cup snipped parsley
¼ cup chopped canned pimiento
1 tablespoon instant minced onion
½ teaspoon salt
  Dash pepper
2 9-ounce packages frozen
  cauliflower, thawed

Mix together condensed soup, eggs, cheese, bread crumbs, parsley, pimiento, onion, salt, and pepper. Add cauliflower and turn into a 10x6x1½-inch baking dish. Bake at 375° till firm, about 45 minutes. Makes 6 to 8 servings.

## Cauliflower with Shrimp Sauce

1 medium head cauliflower, broken
  into flowerets
    • • •
1 10-ounce can frozen condensed
  cream of shrimp soup
½ cup dairy sour cream *or* light
  cream
¼ cup slivered almonds, toasted

Cook flowerets, covered, in small amount of boiling salted water till tender, 10 to 15 minutes; drain cauliflower well.

In a saucepan heat condensed soup over low heat, stirring frequently. Add sour cream *or* light cream; cook and stir just till hot. Add almonds. Pour sauce over hot cauliflowerets. Makes 4 to 6 servings.

**CAVIAR** *(kav′ ē är′)*—The eggs or roe of several species of sturgeon or similar large fish. Caviar is an expensive delicacy that is usually served as an appetizer.

Sturgeon caviar ranges in color from medium gray to black. Caviar is also prepared from the roe of other fish such as whitefish, carp, and codfish. The roe are green, red, or yellow depending on the fish variety. For example, red caviar is the salted eggs of salmon. Black or gray caviar seems to be the type of caviar chosen by most Americans.

Roe vary in size from a pinhead to a small pea. The larger egg is called "beluga," the name of a white sturgeon from the Black and Caspian Seas. A smaller size is given the name "sevruga," also a variety of sturgeon. Caviar enthusiasts may never agree as to which is better, so let your own taste buds be your flavor guide.

In processing caviar, the roe are first washed and sieved to remove membranes and connective tissue. Next, the eggs are lightly salted and then drained. Finally, the caviar is placed in small jars and processed. Once processed, caviar need not be refrigerated until the jar is opened.

Most sturgeon caviar is imported from Russia and Iran where it is usually sold fresh. Fresh caviar is extremely perishable and must be kept iced. Because its holding time is extremely short, imported fresh caviar is very expensive.

Pressed caviar is from the eggs of immature sturgeon as well as those of advanced maturity. Although usually less expensive than the standard fine-granular caviar, pressed caviar is preferred by some gourmets. It makes a fine canapé spread.

Serve caviar icy cold, but not frozen. You chill it right in a container that is nestled in a bed of crushed ice. Also serve small, thin slices of melba or fresh toast along with a selection of accompaniments such as lemon wedges, finely chopped hard-cooked egg white, sieved hard-cooked egg yolk, minced onion, or snipped chives. Spoon caviar onto the toast, then drizzle with lemon juice and sprinkle with the other accompaniments to suit your taste.

For an unusual flavor, serve a little caviar over broiled fish, or mix it into French or Russian salad dressing for a tossed green salad. The connoisseur of caviar prefers it on toast—"straight"—with no additions. In Russia, caviar is spread on black bread or rolled in tiny, thin buckwheat cakes. These tiny roll-ups are then topped with a dollop of sour cream.

## Caviar Appetizers

• Stuff mushroom crowns with caviar.
• Combine cream cheese with red caviar and stuff into celery or artichoke hearts. Or, using a pastry tube, pipe a small amount on crisp rich round crackers.
• Top halved hard-cooked eggs with a tiny amount of caviar and a little minced onion.
• Use as trim for tiny appetizer-size open-face sandwiches.
• Fill miniature cream puffs with caviar.

Trim the top of a folded French omelet with a band of red caviar for a gourmet treat. Sour cream is the accompanying topper.

A simple, yet elegant way to present caviar is nestled in a bed of crushed ice and surrounded with its accompaniments.

## Caviar-Stuffed Eggs

    6 hard-cooked eggs
    2 tablespoons butter or margarine
    1 2-ounce jar (3 tablespoons)
       black caviar

Cut eggs in half lengthwise. Carefully remove and sieve egg yolks. Blend in butter or margarine; carefully stir in caviar and dash pepper. Fill egg whites with yolk mixture. Garnish with parsley, if desired. Makes 12 halves.

**CAYENNE OR RED PEPPER** (*kī en′, kā-*)— A powdery seasoning ground from *Capsicum* pepper pods and seeds. Looking something like paprika, cayenne is not quite as bright in color and is often simply called ground red pepper.

Traditionally there was a difference between cayenne and ground red pepper, cayenne being made from the hottest peppers, while red pepper, not quite as hot, being made from a slightly milder pepper. In the past they were marketed as separate products, but today little distinction is made between the two and many manufacturers even put both names on the label or label the product only red pepper. You can substitute one for the other successfully in most recipes.

The peppers from which cayenne or red pepper is prepared are believed to have had their origin in South America. Today, these peppers are grown in the United States, mainly in Louisiana and South Carolina. They are also imported from Turkey, Japan, Africa, and Mexico.

The process of making cayenne pepper consists of grinding and sifting the dried fruit. Then it is packaged and labeled for the grocery store spice shelf.

Because cayenne is so hot and pungent, use it only in very small amounts to give flavor accent to sauces, cheese or seafood dishes, meat dishes, and eggs. It is also used quite often in both Mexican and Italian dishes. (See also *Spice*.)

**CELERIAC** (*suh ler′ ē ak′*)—A member of the celery family cultivated for its turnip-like root. Other names are celery root, knob celery, and turnip-rooted celery. This low-calorie, winter vegetable is available from October through April.

When shopping for celeriac, choose small-sized roots or knobs since these are best for eating. The large ones tend to be woody and hollow. Because the green top is sparse and inedible, it is usually cut away before the root is marketed. Allow about 1½ pounds for four servings. Store in a cold, moist place.

You must peel the tough outer coat of celeriac before it can be eaten. The peeled root can then be served raw in matchstick strips as an appetizer, or sliced into a salad. If you prefer, it can also be cut up and cooked in water. Dressed with butter or a cream sauce, or mashed, cooked celeriac can be served instead of potatoes on the dinner plate. (See also *Celery*.)

## Marinated Celery Root

*An unusual vegetable prepared very simply—*

Remove and discard green top from 1 medium celery root. Peel root and dice. Cook in boiling water just till tender, about 8 minutes. Drain well. While still warm, cover with French salad dressing. Refrigerate 2 to 3 hours. Serve as an accompaniment with meat or in tomato rosettes as a salad. Makes 4 salad servings.

Shredded carrots add a touch of color and flavor to Celery Slaw. Add this salad to any menu needing something crisp and crunchy.

## Celery Root Sauté

  1 medium celery root
  2 tablespoons butter or margarine
  1 tablespoon snipped parsley

Remove and discard green top from the celery root. Peel root and cut into julienne strips. Cook in boiling salted water just till tender, about 8 minutes; drain.

In small saucepan cook butter till brown. Pour over cooked celery root. Season to taste with salt and pepper. Sprinkle with snipped parsley. Makes 4 servings.

**CELERY**—A vegetable belonging to the parsley family that is eaten raw or cooked.

In early times, wild celery was used for medicinal purposes. Celery still grows wild in some parts of England. It was later domesticated, cultivated, and used as a flavoring agent and a food. The use of celery spread across Europe from Italy to England and France and then to America where commercial growing began in Michigan around the mid-1800's.

*Nutritional value:* As most dieters know, celery is low in calories. Only about three calories can be counted for a small five-inch inner stalk or 17 calories for one cup diced raw celery. It contains some vitamin A—more in the green varieties than in the yellow type. Celery also contains some of the B vitamins.

*Types of celery:* Two types of celery are marketed throughout the year. Formerly, yellow celery (which is bleached white) was the most popular, and some are still marketed as stalks or hearts. But preference in recent years has turned to the pascal or green variety with its large and tender stalks. Pascal celery is almost "stringless."

With either type, a bunch is made up of branches or ribs with leaves. These branches surround the heart. Often the word stalk is used for a branch or rib, as well as for a bunch of celery.

*How to select:* When purchasing celery in the market, look for stalks that are crisp, solid, rigid, and of medium length and thickness. Green leaves that have not been trimmed away should be fresh. Blemishes or decay on outer branches indicate poor quality and the possibility of considerable waste when these outer branches have to be discarded. Avoid bunches of celery with discoloration among the center branches.

*How to store:* After purchasing celery, rinse the stalk well under cold running water to remove any soil. Enclose tightly

Cheese and celery blend together in Creamy Celery Bake. Pimiento and green pepper bits make this a festive-looking dish.

in foil or clear plastic wrap or place in a plastic bag. Store in the crisper of the refrigerator. Celery will keep from one to two weeks if refrigerated properly.

***How to prepare:*** Separate the branches. Cut off leaves and trim roots. Scrub well. Uncooked chopped celery from 8 branches measures about 2¾ cups.

To cook celery, slice outer branches and cut hearts lengthwise. Cook, covered, in a small amount of boiling salted water till just tender, usually for 10 to 15 minutes.

***How to use:*** Celery can be used many ways. Thoroughly scrubbed and trimmed, it is delicious raw as a relish, salad ingredient, or low-calorie snack. Well-washed celery leaves can add flavor to soups, salads, and stews. Celery can be served cooked as a vegetable dish, cooked in a creamy mixture for soup, or added to recipes when a crisp texture is needed, such as in a stuffing for poultry.

Celery appetizers need a minimum amount of preparation. Cut branches in serving-size lengths, then fill branches with a cheese or peanut butter mixture. Or, cut into sticks or fans and serve as go-alongs with creamy, well-seasoned dips.

## Celery Fans

Cut tender celery branches (stalks) in 3- or 4-inch lengths. Make parallel cuts close together from one end *almost* to the other. Or slit both ends almost to the center. (To make fans that curl on top *and* bottom sides, make another cut through strips splitting each in two.) Chill in ice water till strips curl.

## Celery Oriental

Slice 6 to 8 large, outside celery branches (stalks) on the bias. Cook in small amount boiling salted water till just crisp-tender; drain.

In saucepan cook 1 cup sliced fresh mushrooms in 3 tablespoons butter or margarine till tender; add celery and ¼ cup toasted blanched almond halves. Toss lightly over low heat just till vegetable mixture is heated through. (Do not overcook.) Makes 4 to 6 servings.

## Creamy Celery Bake

*A vegetable casserole perfect for company fare—*

      4 cups thinly sliced celery
    ¼ cup butter or margarine
      3 tablespoons all-purpose flour
      1 teaspoon salt
      1 cup milk
              . . .
      1 3-ounce can chopped mushrooms, drained (about ½ cup)
      2 tablespoons chopped green pepper
      2 tablespoons chopped canned pimiento
      4 ounces sharp process American cheese, shredded (1 cup)
              . . .
      1 cup soft bread crumbs
      2 tablespoons butter or margarine, melted

In medium skillet cook celery in ¼ cup butter or margarine till tender, about 5 minutes. Push celery to one side; stir in flour and salt. Add milk all at once; cook and stir till mixture thickens and bubbles.

Stir in mushrooms, green pepper, and pimiento. Add cheese and stir till melted. Turn mixture into 10x6x1½-inch baking dish. Combine bread crumbs and the 2 tablespoons melted butter. Sprinkle over casserole. Bake at 350° for 20 minutes. Makes about 8 servings.

## Celery Slaw

*Goes especially well with poultry or fish—*

      1 tablespoon sugar
    ½ teaspoon salt
    ¼ teaspoon paprika
    ⅛ teaspoon pepper
      2 tablespoons salad oil
      1 tablespoon wine vinegar
    ⅓ cup dairy sour cream
              . . .
      3 cups thinly sliced celery
    ½ cup shredded carrot

Combine sugar, salt, paprika, pepper, salad oil, and vinegar. Slowly stir into sour cream. Add to celery and carrot in a bowl. Toss lightly to mix. Makes about 6 servings.

## Speedy Celery Stuffing

  1  7- or 8-ounce package herb-
     seasoned stuffing mix
  1  teaspoon ground sage
  1  cup chopped celery
  ½  cup chopped onion
  ¼  cup butter or margarine
1¼  cups chicken broth

To stuffing mix add sage, celery, and onion.
Add butter to chicken broth; heat. Add broth
mixture to stuffing. Toss lightly. Use as a stuffing for two 4- to 5-pound chickens or one 10-
pound turkey. Makes about 6 cups stuffing.

## Cream of Celery Soup

1½  cups diced celery
  ⅓  cup chopped onion

      • • •

  2  tablespoons butter or margarine
  2  tablespoons all-purpose flour
  ½  teaspoon salt
  3  cups milk
    Butter or margarine

Cook celery and onion, covered, in 1 cup boiling
salted water till tender, about 13 minutes.

Meanwhile, prepare white sauce by melting 2
tablespoons butter in saucepan over low heat.
Stir in flour, salt, and dash white pepper. Add
milk all at once. Cook quickly, stirring constantly till mixture thickens and bubbles. Stir
into cooked celery and liquid. Heat through.
Season to taste with salt and pepper. Top servings with butter. Makes 6 servings.

Dried celery flakes for use as seasoning are available on the spice and herb
shelves in most supermarkets. One tablespoon celery flakes equals two tablespoons
fresh chopped celery. (See also *Vegetable.*)

**CELERY CABBAGE**—Alternate name for Chinese Cabbage. (See also *Chinese Cabbage.*)

**CELERY SALT**—A blend of table salt and
ground celery seed. Used primarily as a
seasoning, it is particularly good with poultry, fish, in soups, and mixed with tomato
juice as an appetizer. (See also *Salt.*)

## Herb Fried Chicken

½  teaspoon dried thyme leaves,
    crushed
½  teaspoon dried marjoram leaves,
    crushed
½  teaspoon celery salt
1  2½- to 3-pound ready-to-cook
    broiler-fryer chicken, cut up
⅓  cup all-purpose flour
3  tablespoons shortening

Combine thyme, marjoram, celery salt, 1 teaspoon salt, and ¼ teaspoon pepper. Sprinkle
over chicken. Roll chicken in flour. Slowly
brown chicken pieces in melted shortening,
about 15 minutes, being careful not to crowd
pieces in skillet. Reduce heat. Cover and cook
till tender, 30 to 40 minutes, uncovering skillet
last 10 minutes of cooking. Makes 4 servings.

**CELERY SEED**—The small, olive brown
seeds of a wild variety of celery called
smallage. The whole seeds lend a celery-
like flavor to salad dressings, homemade
potato salads, soups, stews, cabbage cole-
slaws, relishes, and pickles.

## Patio Potato Salad

⅓  cup sugar
1  tablespoon cornstarch
½  cup milk
¼  cup vinegar
1  egg
¼  cup butter or margarine
¾  teaspoon celery seed
¼  teaspoon dry mustard
¼  cup chopped onion
¼  cup mayonnaise or salad dressing
7  medium potatoes, cooked,
    peeled, and diced
3  hard-cooked eggs, chopped
   Paprika

In saucepan combine sugar and cornstarch; add
next 6 ingredients and ¾ teaspoon salt. Cook
and stir over low heat till bubbly. Remove from
heat; add onion and mayonnaise. Cool. Combine potatoes and hard-cooked eggs; gently fold
in dressing. Chill. Just before serving sprinkle
with paprika. Makes 6 servings.

**CELLOPHANE NOODLES**—Very slender, white, translucent, round noodles made from powdered mung beans or pea starch. Dried and sold in skeins, these noodles are used in Chinese cookery. Cellophane noodles, sometimes called bean thread, are available in oriental grocery stores.

The noodles have very little flavor of their own but will absorb the flavor of the broth or liquid in which they are cooked. Another favorite way to use them is as a crisp garnish for stir-fried dishes. The loosened skein of dried noodles is fried quickly in deep fat.

**CELLULOSE**—A carbohydrate that is the chief material found in the cell walls of plants. In addition to providing the structural framework for all fruits and vegetables, cellulose is present in the shells of legumes and both the outer layer and inner cellwork of cereal grains.

Although not considered digestible except if from young tender produce, cellulose is an important contributor of bulk or roughage to the diet and is necessary to maintain body regularity.

**CEPE** *(sehp)*—A large, fleshy mushroom found in France. The cap measures six or more inches in diameter and ranges from yellow to reddish brown in color. Its flavor is usually more pronounced than that of American cultivated mushrooms.

**CEREAL**—1. Edible seed of grains. 2. Grasses that produce the grains. 3. Manufactured products made from grains. Wheat, corn, rice, oats, rye, and barley are the most common cereal grains. Although not cereal grains, buckwheat and soybean products are sometimes used as cereals or blended with cereal mixtures.

The word cereal comes from an ancient Roman festival known as the *Cerealia*. It originated about 500 B.C. and honored Ceres, the goddess of grain. This springtime ceremony sought the goddess's protection for the coming crop.

Grain was not the only food, but it was so basic to life that measures of grain became one of the earliest forms of money. In Mesopotamia, both grain and silver were used as legal tender.

Kernels of different cereal grains will vary in size and shape. However, their basic structure is similar; each contains the bran, the endosperm, and the germ. The thin outer layers, called bran, serve as a protective covering. The tender endosperm which constitutes approximately 85 percent of the kernel, contains the food supply for the growing plant. The third segment is the germ or embryo.

Many of the types of grains you eat today were cultivated in prehistoric times. Stone Age peoples ate roasted grains, and pounded some between stones to make a flour. As long ago as 3000 B.C., rice was grown and used in the Orient, and corn was eaten in the Americas by the Aztecs. While no exact date is recorded, barley and wheat are known to have been cultivated and used long before oats and rye.

By the time of the ancient Egyptians, Greeks, and Romans, grain cultivation was quite highly developed, as was grinding or milling. The Romans developed a mill that could be turned by men or animals, and they, as well as the Egyptians, developed methods for sieving their grains to remove coarse chaff. Later came the use of water wheels and power mills.

Today, much of this work is done by great, modern, electrically powered grain mills with roller-crusher devices and machines for hulling and refining grains.

*Nutritional value:* Cereal in all its forms plays an important role in man's diet by providing good nutrition at a relatively low cost. Milling and processing affect the amounts of nutrients in the final cereal product purchased by the homemaker. Label information on each package gives details about the specific food.

Whole-grain cereals along with restored or enriched cereals are good sources of iron, phosphorus, and the B vitamins, thiamine and niacin. They are, however, low in vitamin C and, unless enriched, vitamin D also. Only yellow corn contains vitamin A in any significant amount.

In their natural state, cereal grain products provide energy in the form of carbohydrate. Fat is a minor component. Although cereal protein is abundant and economical, it is more useful to the body

**Cereal terms to know**

*Whole grain cereal* is a grain product which has retained the specific nutrients of the natural grain before it was processed. It also contains the bran, the germ, and the endosperm in their natural proportions.

*Restored cereal* is made from either the entire grain or portions of one or more grains to which sufficient amounts of thiamine, niacin, and iron have been added to match the levels of these nutrients found in the whole grain before processing.

*Enriched cereal* is one to which vitamins and minerals have been added in amounts beyond the quantities which are naturally present in the whole grain.

when combined with other protein sources. Milk, a natural serving partner, is the perfect nutritional complement.

Besides the protein boost, milk supplements the calcium and riboflavin present. When the milk is fortified with vitamins A and D, the nutritional score for the combination is even higher. The nutritional value of milk is enhanced by the partnership, too. Nutrients present in smaller amounts in milk, such as thiamine, niacin, and iron, are present in larger amounts in cereal. This highly nutritious partnership holds true whether the milk used is whole or skim. The only difference is that the milk fat (butterfat) in whole milk will increase the fat content and caloric value of the final serving.

***Types of cereal:*** These nutritionally necessary foods are generally grouped according to whether the cereal is served hot or cold. Farina, oatmeal, whole wheat, rolled wheat cereals and some grain combinations are in the group to be served hot. The cold cereals include precooked crisp flakes, puffs, shredded biscuits of various sizes, and many grain combinations.

Hot cereals require varying amounts of cooking depending on the processing the grains have received. Each cereal product has its own characteristic flavor and texture. For additional variety, maple, malt, or chocolate flavorings may be added to some cereals by processors before being placed on the market.

Cereals labeled quick cooking are processed in thinner, smaller particles that cook more rapidly than the regular version of the grain. Several are marketed in instant form and need only the addition of boiling water to provide a serving of hot, nourishing cereal.

Cold cereals are crisp, ready-to-eat favorites that appear on the breakfast table in a wondrous assortment of shapes and flavors. They are flaked, shredded, puffed, popped, or formed into intriguing shapes designed to delight the youngsters, who consume them in great quantities. Many cereals are presweetened which makes them good snack food as well as breakfast food. Raisins or special flavorings packed with the cereal add to the fun.

***How to store:*** Both dry or uncooked cereals are best stored tightly covered in a cool, dry place. Most ready-to-eat cereals are packaged with an innerlining between carton and food. Care in opening and reclosing both package and lining will help maintain freshness throughout storage.

Generous spoonfuls of melting Honey Butter enhance piping hot bowls of Whole Wheat for breakfast. Pass milk, if desired.

***How to use:*** Breakfast is, by far, the meal at which cereal is most frequently served. The crisp ready-to-eat favorites are poured from the package into a bowl and topped with milk, fruit, and sugar, if desired. Brown sugar, honey, or one of the flavored pancake syrups can be substituted for the sugar as a special treat. Hot cereals take only minutes to prepare and can be dressed up with fruit and syrups in much the same way as their crisp counterparts.

Cereals have many uses as cooking ingredients. Rice and oats can be blended with meat mixtures when preparing loaves and casseroles to help stretch the meat servings and to improve the texture of the finished dish. Crushed flakes may be used in burgers from time to time, but they are at their best as a crusty coating for fish and chicken or as a quick topping for baked main dishes. Barley and rice are favorites in soups or served with creamed foods and in casseroles.

Cereals are no strangers in cookies, desserts, and quick breads where their nut-like crunch adds flavor and texture.

(See *Grain* and individual cereals for additional information.)

## Hot Whole Wheat and Honey Butter

½ cup butter or margarine
¼ cup honey
  Ready-to-cook whole wheat cereal

Prepare Honey Butter by whipping butter till fluffy. Slowly add honey, beating until smooth.

Prepare 4 servings of ready-to-cook whole wheat cereal according to package directions. Spoon into bowls. Top with Honey Butter.

## Spicy Raisin Oatmeal

Bring 3½ cups cold water to a brisk boil. Add 1 cup seedless raisins, 1 teaspoon salt, 1 teaspoon ground cinnamon, and ½ teaspoon ground nutmeg. Slowly stir in 1½ cups quick-cooking rolled oats, making sure water continues to boil. Reduce heat; cook 5 minutes, stirring occasionally. Remove from heat; cover oatmeal and let stand 5 minutes. Serve hot with sugar and cream or milk. Makes 4 servings.

## Cerealsnaps

*Crisp goodies to fill the cookie jar—*

½ cup butter or margarine
½ cup brown sugar
½ cup granulated sugar
1 egg
1 teaspoon vanilla
1¼ cups sifted all-purpose flour
½ teaspoon baking powder
½ teaspoon baking soda
½ teaspoon salt
2 cups crisp rice cereal
1 3½-ounce can flaked coconut
  (1⅓ cups)

Cream butter with sugars; add egg and vanilla, creaming till fluffy. Sift together dry ingredients; stir into creamed mixture. Stir in cereal and coconut. Shape in ¾-inch balls; place about 2½ inches apart on *ungreased* cookie sheet. Bake at 350° till lightly browned, about 10 minutes. Cool slightly; remove from pan. Cool on rack. Makes 5 dozen cookies.

## Crunchy Date Rounds

*Sugared flakes add crunch to tender date cookies—*

½ cup butter or margarine
½ cup granulated sugar
¼ cup brown sugar
1 egg
1 teaspoon vanilla
1 cup sifted all-purpose flour
½ teaspoon baking powder
¼ teaspoon baking soda
½ teaspoon salt
½ cup chopped walnuts
1 cup snipped pitted dates
1½ cups presweetened cereal flakes,
  coarsely crushed

Combine butter, sugars, egg, and vanilla; beat well. Sift together flour, baking powder, soda, and salt; gradually add to creamed mixture, blending well. Stir in nuts and dates. Drop from teaspoon into crushed cereal flakes, rolling to coat well. Bake about 2 inches apart on *ungreased* cookie sheet at 375° till top springs back when lightly touched, about 10 to 12 minutes. Makes 3 dozen.

Pass the Scramble at snack time or whenever coffee or iced beverages are served. It is a zippy concoction of mixed nuts, pretzel sticks, and a multitude of crisp ready-to-eat cereals.

## Scramble

- 2 pounds mixed salted nuts
- 1 11-ounce package spoon-size shredded-wheat biscuits
- 1 10½-ounce package doughnut-shaped oat cereal
- 1 6-ounce package bite-size shredded rice squares
- 1 7-ounce package small pretzel twists
- 1 5¾-ounce package slim pretzel sticks
- 1 4½-ounce can pretzel bits
- 2 cups salad oil
- 2 tablespoons Worcestershire sauce
- 1 tablespoon garlic salt
- 1 teaspoon seasoned salt

Mix first 7 ingredients in large pan or roaster. Combine remaining ingredients; pour over cereal mixture. Bake at 250° for 2 hours, stirring and turning mixture with wooden spoon every 15 minutes (do not crush). Makes 9 quarts.

## Berry-Cereal Parfaits

- 1 quart vanilla ice cream
- 2 10-ounce packages frozen sliced strawberries, partially thawed
- 2 cups presweetened cornflakes

In each tall parfait glass, layer about ¼ cup ice cream, about 3 tablespoons strawberries, and ¼ cup cornflakes. Top with another ¼ cup ice cream. Garnish with berries. Serves 8.

## Easy Italian Chicken

*Oven baked with a crispy, garlic-flavored crust—*

    1 2½- to 3-pound ready-to-cook
      broiler-fryer chicken, cut up
    ½ cup butter or margarine,
      softened
    ½ envelope garlic salad dressing
      mix (1 tablespoon)
    1 cup cornflake crumbs
      Paprika

Pat chicken pieces dry with paper towels. Thoroughly combine softened butter or margarine and salad dressing mix. Using a spatula, spread butter mixture over chicken pieces. Roll in cornflake crumbs. Sprinkle chicken lightly with paprika.

In a shallow pan arrange chicken pieces skin side up making sure that they do not touch one another. Bake at 375° until tender, about 1 hour. It is not necessary to turn the pieces. Makes 4 servings.

## Mock Indian Pudding

*Crushed cornflakes replace cornmeal in this version of a traditional New England dessert—*

    2 slightly beaten eggs
    ½ cup light molasses
    ¼ cup sugar
    1 tablespoon butter or margarine,
      melted
    ½ teaspoon ground cinnamon
    ¼ teaspoon salt
    ¼ teaspoon ground cloves
            •  •  •
    3 cups milk
    4 cups cornflakes, coarsely
      crushed
    1 pint vanilla ice cream

Combine eggs, molasses, sugar, melted butter, cinnamon, salt, and cloves; mix well. Stir in milk and cornflake crumbs. Pour into greased 1½-quart casserole. Place in shallow pan on oven rack; pour hot water into pan till 1-inch deep. Bake at 350° till knife inserted halfway between center and edge comes out clean, about 1 hour. Serve pudding warm, topped with ice cream. Makes 6 servings.

## Peachy Rice Pudding

    1 cup uncooked packaged
      precooked rice
    1 cup milk
    2 tablespoons butter or margarine
    1 16-ounce can peach slices,
      undrained
    2 beaten eggs
      Dash ground nutmeg

In saucepan combine rice and milk; bring to boiling. Cover; reduce heat and cook 5 minutes. Stir in butter, peaches, eggs, and nutmeg. Cook and stir 2 minutes more. Sprinkle with additional nutmeg. Serve with cream. Serves 4.

## Crunch Sticks

    1 package refrigerated biscuits
      (10 biscuits)
      Milk
    1 cup crisp rice cereal,
      coarsely crushed
    1 tablespoon caraway, celery,
      or dillseed

Cut biscuits in half. Roll each piece into 4-inch pencil-like stick. Brush with milk. Mix cereal crumbs, seed, and 1 teaspoon salt in shallow pan (be sure salt is well distributed). Roll sticks in cereal mixture. Place on greased baking sheet; bake at 450° till lightly browned, about 8 to 10 minutes. Makes 20 sticks.

**CHAFING DISH**—Cooking equipment consisting of a deep metal pan with a handle, a container for water, and a heat source in a frame to support the two pans. The unit may be of modern design and material or of classic silver; in any case, chafing dishes are used at the table to cook foods or to keep them warm.

The cooking pan is called a blazer and the water basin a bain-marie. Together they function as a double boiler for preparing sauces or holding foods at serving temperature. The blazer pan alone can be used like a skillet directly over the heat.

Portable heating equipment, while currently popular, is by no means new. The early Babylonians and Egyptians used braziers as space heaters to take the chill out of a room. Over the centuries the design changed and these little stoves on legs moved from floor to tabletop. Cooking became their chief function. A further improvement occurred when crude versions of the double boiler were used on the little stoves. They were clumsy at first, and it was only natural that a single piece of equipment should evolve.

Over the years chafing dishes became more elegant. For example, silversmiths in Europe and later in colonial America did a good business making chafing dishes for use in the finest homes. Chafing dishes were extremely practical. In large homes the kitchen was often a great distance from the dining area. Foods in chafing dishes could be kept hot in the dining room until everyone was served.

Credit for many of the refinements in the chafing dish and the cookery for which it is used goes to Alexis Soyer, a Frenchman of remarkable talent. He lived in the nineteenth century and built his reputation as chef at the Reform Club, the London headquarters for a gourmet society. He was not only a superb cook, but also an inventor and cook book writer.

Because he delighted in preparing delicate sauces in the same room in which the dishes were served, his adaptations of the burner and his use of the water bath made possible this elegant food.

Chafing dishes have long been considered essential in fine restaurants where cooking spectacular dishes at the diner's own table is a specialty of the house. Now they are becoming popular for home entertaining as well. No matter how simple, chafing-dish food looks glamorous, and the hostess spends less time in the kitchen —more with her guests.

***How to use a chafing dish:*** This versatile piece of equipment fills many serving needs. Sometimes, hot appetizer dips or one-dish meals are completely prepared in the kitchen, then transferred to the chafing dish to keep hot at the table. In this case the water pan is used to distribute the heat evenly over the bottom of the blazer. Egg-yolk sauces and cheese rarebits are also cooked over hot water.

The blazer pan alone lends itself to the preparation of simple food such as scrambled eggs. It is also used for glamorous foods flamed at the table such as Cherries Jubilee, Crepes Suzette, and Steak Diane.

For actual cooking at the table, most hostesses prefer heat that can be adjusted. Chafing dishes are usually equipped with either an alcohol burner or a container for canned heat. The alcohol burner uses denatured alcohol which can be purchased at a hardware store. The burner has a lever or regulator by which the intensity of the flame can be adjusted. On the other hand, when canned heat is used, the holder should have a sliding lid so that the amount of flame exposed can be increased or decreased to suit the food.

Candles, used in some types of food warmers, do not give off enough heat for cooking in a chafing dish.

Table-side cookery should be the spectacular result of careful planning and preparation. The secret is to have everything ready before guests arrive.

Choose speedy recipes for chafing dish cookery. The dish may require several ingredients, but cooking time and cooking

Wreathed in cheese, chopped onion, and olives, a peppy Sombrero Spread awaits the dipping of a crisp tostada or corn chip.

steps at the table should be kept to a minimum. For example, if the sauce for a curry should take more than a few minutes to prepare, make it in advance, pour it into the chafing dish, and add the last few ingredients at the table.

Sometimes it is faster to brown the meat in a skillet on the range in the kitchen, then transfer to the chafing dish for final assembly or cooking at the table. (See *Cherries Jubilee, Crepes, Steak Diane, Stroganoff* for additional information.)

## Sombrero Spread

    ½ pound ground beef
    ½ cup chopped onion
    ¼ cup hot-style catsup
    ½ teaspoon chili powder
    ½ teaspoon salt
    1 8-ounce can undrained red
        kidney beans
    2 ounces sharp process American
        cheese, shredded (½ cup)
    ¼ cup chopped pimiento-stuffed
        green olives
        Tostadas

In 8-inch skillet or blazer pan of chafing dish, cook meat and ¼ *cup* of the onion till meat is brown. Stir in catsup, chili powder, and salt. Add beans; mash mixture very well. Heat through. Garnish with cheese, olives, and remaining onion. Place over hot water to keep warm. Serve with tostadas. Makes 2 cups.

## Easy Cheese Dunk

    ½ 10½-ounce can condensed cream
        of mushroom soup
    2 6-ounce rolls garlic-flavored
        cheese food, cut up
    3 tablespoons dry sherry
    1 teaspoon Worcestershire sauce
    ⅛ to ¼ teaspoon bottled hot
        pepper sauce

In saucepan or blazer pan of chafing dish, combine soup and cheese food. Heat over very low heat till cheese melts, stirring often to blend. Add remaining ingredients. Keep hot for dipping. Makes about 2 cups.

## Sweet-and-Sour Surprises

    2 tablespoons cornstarch
    2 tablespoons sugar
    1 chicken bouillon cube, crumbled
    1 cup pineapple juice
    ½ cup water
    ⅓ cup vinegar
    2 tablespoons soy sauce
    1 tablespoon butter or margarine
    ½ pound tiny meatballs, cooked
    ½ pound shrimp, cooked
    ½ pound chicken livers, cooked

Combine cornstarch, sugar, and bouillon cube. Add pineapple juice, water, vinegar, soy sauce, and butter or margarine. Cook and stir till thick and bubbly. Cover; simmer 5 minutes longer. Transfer to blazer pan of chafing dish. Group meatballs, shrimp, and livers in sauce. Heat through. Set pan over bain-marie; serve hot with cocktail picks. Makes 1½ cups sauce.

## Easy Shrimp Sauté

    6 tablespoons butter or margarine
    1 clove garlic, minced
    1½ pounds shelled raw
        shrimp (3 cups)
    ¼ cup dry sherry
    2 tablespoons snipped parsley
        Hot cooked rice

Melt butter in blazer pan of chafing dish or skillet; add garlic and cook slightly. Add shrimp; cook, stirring frequently, till shrimp are tender and turn pink, about 5 minutes. Stir in wine and parsley. Heat to boiling. Serve with rice. Makes 4 to 6 servings.

## Beef and Lima Skillet

Cook one 10-ounce package frozen lima beans according to package directions; drain. In skillet or blazer pan of chafing dish brown 1 pound ground beef. Combine ½ clove garlic, minced; 1 tablespoon cornstarch; 1 tablespoon sugar; 2 tablespoons soy sauce; 1 teaspoon prepared horseradish; ½ cup water; and few drops bottled hot pepper sauce. Add to meat. Cook till thick and bubbly. Add limas; cook and stir till heated through. Makes 6 servings.

## Creamed Mushrooms

>     6 tablespoons butter or margarine
>     ½ pound fresh mushrooms, sliced
>          (3 cups)
>     3 tablespoons all-purpose flour
>     2 cups milk
>     1 tablespoon soy sauce
>     ¼ teaspoon salt
>          Dash pepper
>          Toast cups

Melt butter in skillet. Add sliced mushrooms; cook gently till tender and lightly browned. Push mushrooms to one side of pan; blend in flour. Add milk all at once. Cook and stir till mushroom mixture thickens and bubbles.

Add soy sauce, salt, and pepper. Transfer to chafing dish and keep warm over hot water. Serve in toast cups. Makes 4 servings.

To prepare *Toast Cups:* Trim crusts from 4 slices white bread. Spread bread with ¼ cup softened butter or margarine. Carefully press into *ungreased* medium muffin cups. Toast at 350° for about 15 minutes. Makes 4 toast cups.

## Mock Stroganoff

>     1 pound ground beef
>     ¼ cup chopped onion
>     2 tablespoons all-purpose flour
>     1 teaspoon sugar
>     ½ teaspoon salt
>     ½ teaspoon dried basil leaves,
>          crushed
>     ⅛ teaspoon garlic powder
>     ⅛ teaspoon pepper
>     1 10½-ounce can condensed
>          beef broth
>     1 6-ounce can tomato paste
>     1 3-ounce can sliced mushrooms,
>          drained (½ cup)
>     1 cup dairy sour cream
>          Hot buttered noodles

In skillet or blazer pan of chafing dish cook meat and onion till meat is lightly browned. Combine flour, sugar, salt, basil, garlic powder, and pepper; sprinkle over meat. Stir in broth and tomato paste. Simmer, uncovered, 10 minutes, stirring occasionally. Stir in mushrooms and sour cream. Heat, but *do not boil.* Serve over noodles. Makes 6 servings.

## Company Creamed Tuna

>     2 tablespoons finely chopped
>          onion
>     3 tablespoons butter
>     3 tablespoons all-purpose flour
>     ¼ teaspoon salt
>          Dash pepper
>     1¼ cups milk
>     ½ cup dairy sour cream
>     1 6½- or 7-ounce can tuna,
>          drained
>     3 tablespoons dry white wine
>     2 tablespoons snipped parsley
>          Toasted slivered almonds
>          Pastry shells *or* buttered
>          toast points

In blazer pan of chafing dish cook onion in butter till tender but not brown. Blend in flour, salt, and pepper. Add milk all at once; cook quickly, stirring constantly, until mixture thickens and bubbles. Stir in sour cream. Add tuna, wine, and parsley. Heat through. Set blazer pan on top of bain-marie over flame. Sprinkle toasted almonds over sauce. Spoon into pastry shells or over hot buttered toast points. Makes 4 servings.

## Curried-Egg Biscuits

>     1 package refrigerated biscuits
>          (10 biscuits)
>     ¼ cup shortening
>     1 tablespoon finely chopped onion
>     3 tablespoons all-purpose flour
>     1 teaspoon salt
>     1 teaspoon curry powder
>     ½ teaspoon sugar
>     2½ cups milk
>     1 8-ounce can peas, drained
>     6 hard-cooked eggs, sliced

Bake biscuits according to package directions. Meanwhile, melt shortening in blazer pan of chafing dish or in a saucepan. Add onion and cook till tender but not brown. Blend in flour, salt, curry powder, and sugar, stirring till smooth. Add milk all at once. Cook, stirring constantly, till mixture thickens and bubbles. Add drained peas and egg slices. Heat till mixture is hot through. Split hot biscuits. Spoon curried mixture over biscuits. Makes 5 servings.

**CHALLAH**—The traditional Jewish Sabbath bread or twist. The loaf is leavened with yeast and has a velvety crumb. The dough gets its golden color from the addition of eggs and sometimes saffron. The loaf is usually braided and the top brushed with egg just before baking.

**CHAMPAGNE**—A sparkling white wine produced in the Champagne region of France, northeast of Paris. High-quality sparkling white and pink champagne wines are also produced in the United States. Vintage champagne, either domestic or imported, is wine that has been made from grapes which were grown all in the same year. Although vineyards and winemaking had been known in France since Roman times, it was a legendary Benedictine monk who in the late 1600's developed a method for capturing the "devil's wine." This was the local name for wine that formed a gas during aging and burst forth from the bottle. Dom Pérignon determined that the sparkle in the bubbly wine was carbon dioxide and devised a way to cork the bottle securely to hold the bubbles in. This knowledgeable man is also credited with establishing methods of mixing or blending wines for highest quality.

***How champagne is produced:*** Climate, variety of grapes, and careful tending of the vine determine the quality of the final wine. The right amount of sun at the right time during the growing season to develop the flavor and sugar content of the grape influences the quality and handling of the wine at every stage of processing. At the right moment of ripeness, the grapes are harvested, and the juice pressed, mixed with the sugar if needed, and allowed to ferment. During fermentation the sugars are changed to alcohol and carbon dioxide is formed. Development of this new wine is carefully watched at each stage. It is bottled in the spring when the right amount of fermentation has been achieved.

Champagne and sparkling wines receive a second fermentation. It is this second process which gives the wine its sparkle. At the time the new wine is bottled, a yeast culture and syrup are added. The wine is allowed to age for three to four years. But it is not forgotten. During these many months the bottles of wine are placed cork-side down in racks and turned gently at regular intervals so that any sediment in the wine will collect and settle at the neck of the bottle.

Finally, it is time to remove the temporary cork along with the collected sediment. The disgorging, as it is called, must be done very rapidly and carefully so that a minimum of wine comes out with the sediment. Over the years several techniques have been used, but today many wine producers accomplish the disgorging by freezing only the neck of the inverted bottle. When the cork is removed, the pressure of the gas inside the wine will push out the frozen sediment.

Any lost wine is quickly replaced with wine from another bottle containing wine from the same year or a blend designed to produce the desired flavor and quality. If sweetness is desired, it is added at this point. Then, the new cork is set firmly down into the bottle. The final step is to wire it tightly into place.

According to the amount of sweetness, the wine will be *brut* (very dry), *extra dry*, or *demi sec* (fairly sweet). When no sweetening is added, the wine is designated *natural: Brut* is the most popular.

In the United States a bulk method for the making of champagne also has been developed. It is a less expensive process and the finished wine is therefore less costly. The second period of fermentation takes place in the closed tank. When the champagne is ready to be bottled, it is filtered and bottled under pressure to preserve the precious bubbles. When champagne is prepared by the bulk process, the label will so state.

***How to serve champagne:*** It is a festive wine served chilled, but not icy cold. There are two satisfactory methods for chilling champagne. You can place the bottle in the refrigerator for about an hour or let it stand about 15 minutes in an ice bucket. Whichever method is chosen, be careful to avoid shaking the bottle.

To remove the cork with a minimum loss of champagne when it "pops," carefully loosen the wire fastener, keeping **a** thumb over the cork. Rest the bottle on the table while loosening the wire; you'll have better control of the situation.

Then pick up the bottle in one hand and grasp the cork in the other; twist the bottle rather than the cork. There will be a resounding pop when it slips out, but the outpouring wine is easily captured if you keep a wine glass handy.

At one time the shallow saucer champagne glass—with or without a hollow stem—was prized for serving champagne. Now the eight-ounce tulip-shaped glass is a popular choice, but the all-purpose wine glass will do nicely, too.

Because of its sparkle, and its reputation as a beverage for celebrations, champagne is often used in punch or cocktails at receptions. Many hostesses enjoy serving champagne when entertaining at brunch. (See also *Wines and Spirits*.)

## Orange Champagne Cocktail

    1 4/5 pint bottle (1¾ cups)
        champagne, chilled
    2 7-ounce bottles ginger ale,
        chilled (about 2 cups)
    1 cup orange juice, chilled
        Fresh strawberries, washed,
        hulled, and sliced

Combine beverages in pitcher. Serve in glasses with a few strawberry slices. Serves 6 to 8.

## Cold Duck

For each serving, combine one part chilled champagne and one part chilled sparkling burgundy in a champagne glass.

**CHAMPIGNON** *(sham pin' yuhn)* — The French word for mushroom, particularly edible field varieties.

**CHAPATI** *(cuh pa' tē)*—The handmade flat bread of India prepared from whole wheat flour and water. The unleavened dough is first patted into a paper-thin, flat pancake which resembles the Mexican tortilla and then it is baked on a hot griddle.

## Chapati

    2 cups sifted all-purpose flour
    ¼ cup salad oil
    7 tablespoons water

Sift together flour and 1 teaspoon salt. Add oil, mixing well with hands. (Dough will be very stiff.) Knead 5 to 7 minutes till dough has satiny appearance. Pinch off pieces of dough about 1½ inches in diameter. Roll each to 6-inch circle. Brown on both sides on lightly greased hot griddle. Dot with butter or margarine, if desired. Makes about 1 dozen.

**CHANUKAH**—Hanukkah, the Jewish Festival of Lights celebrated late in December. (See also *Hanukkah*.)

**CHAPON**—A crusty piece of French bread well rubbed with a cut clove of garlic, then tossed with salad greens. The chapon is discarded before the salad is served. Thus, you add the flavor of garlic without adding pieces of garlic. Chapon is also the French word designating a capon.

Chapaties, lightly browned and hot from the griddle, are traditional accompaniments for the pungent curries served in India.

**CHARCOAL**—A black substance obtained by heating or partially burning organic matter. This organic matter can be certain animal or vegetable substances such as bones or, most often, wood. Large pieces smolder in the presence of little air so the volatile matter is removed. This produces an impure carbon product which is porous and lightweight.

Charcoal has a number of properties that are used in the manufacture or preparation of foods. It removes coloring from liquids, absorbs gases, and gives off intense heat when burned.

Charcoal is used as a purifying agent, both commercially and in the home. As a commercial agent, it is used to filter out the color in wines and liqueurs, to decolorize beet-sugar juices, and to purify water and absorb odors if present. In the house, homemakers can place lumps of charcoal in the refrigerator to absorb any unpleasant odors.

Charcoal is best known and most often used in the home as a fuel for barbecuing foods. It produces a cleaner, more intense heat than wood does, and it is compact, lightweight, and easy to store.

Either briquets or lumps are used in barbecuing. Briquets are made from ground charcoal which is pressed into uniform blocks. Because of their uniformity, briquets provide more even heat. Lumps ignite and are ready for cooking faster, but they burn out faster than briquets.

Briquets and lumps are sold in 5-, 10-, 20-, and 40-pound sacks. Some have a self-starting feature, and some add a hickory or other special flavor to the food.

Store charcoal in a dry place to protect it from the moisture in the air. And be sure you are using it in a well-ventilated area, for burning charcoal gives off carbon monoxide. Start the fire with an electric starter if one is available and an outlet is nearby, or start with liquid starter and

### Glowing red coals in a hurry

←Building a fire with charcoal briquets and an electric fire starter is simple—just rest the element in coals for a few minutes.

matches. Self-starting charcoal is lighted simply by putting a match to it. Charcoal can be used a second time if allowed to dry thoroughly after the fire has been smothered or doused. (See also *Barbecue*.)

**CHARD**—A variety of the beet, also called Swiss chard. Its large green leaves and white, succulent stalks have a mild flavor reminiscent of asparagus. The root is not used in cooking.

Chard is a rich source of vitamin A; it has some vitamin C, iron, and B vitamins. A serving averages 20 calories.

This vegetable is most likely to be found in the markets during summer and fall months, though it's not commonly stocked. Those who are especially fond of chard can easily grow it in home gardens.

When selecting chard, choose tender, green leaves and crisp stalks. One pound makes two servings. Store in crisper of the refrigerator and use within two days.

To prepare chard, wash it several times and cut into pieces. Boil till tender, about 10 to 20 minutes; drain and season. Salt and pepper, butter, and lemon juice are good flavor accents. The stalk can also be sautéed. Leaves can be cooked like spinach or used in soups. (See also *Vegetable*.)

**CHARLOTTE** (*shär′ luht*)—A dessert with a sweet filling surrounded by cake or bread. The typical charlotte is made in a mold lined with cake or thin, crisp bread and filled with a fruit, whipped cream, or custard mixture. It is usually served cold, although the oldest variety, apple charlotte, is served hot. (See also *Dessert*.)

**CHARLOTTE RUSSE** (*shär luht rōōs′*)—A well-chilled charlotte made with sponge cake or ladyfingers and filled with any flavor of Bavarian cream.

The creation of this dessert is credited to Carême (1783-1833), the illustrious French cook. He first made it for high-ranking Frenchmen and foreign dignitaries. The name was charlotte parisienne originally. Later it became known as charlotte russe in honor of Czar Alexander I.

In the 1920's this dessert gained in popularity. The charlotte russe became much easier to mold and keep well chilled with the introduction of the refrigerators in the home. Convenience products have made the charlotte even easier to prepare today. You needn't bake the sponge cake or ladyfingers—buy them. Instead of making Bavarian cream, choose from a wide variety of pudding mixes for a quick filling.

This elegant dessert deserves decorations of whipped cream, fresh fruit, glacé fruit, or even candied flowers.

Serve it any time of the day. Dessert is always special when it's charlotte russe with coffee or tea. (See also *Dessert*.)

## Chocolate Charlotte Russe

1 4½- or 5-ounce package *regular*
    vanilla pudding mix
1 teaspoon unflavored gelatin
2 cups milk
1 4-ounce bar sweet baking
    chocolate
1½ cups whipping cream
2 3-ounce packages
    ladyfingers, split

In saucepan combine pudding mix and gelatin; stir in milk. Cook and stir over medium heat till mixture boils. Remove from heat. Break choc-

Line dish generously with waxed paper, so charlotte russe can be lifted out easily without disturbing the frame of ladyfingers.

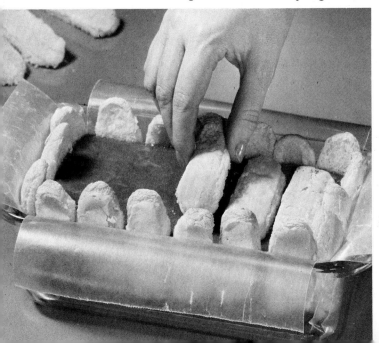

olate into squares and add to hot pudding mixture. Stir till chocolate is melted. Cool completely; then beat till pudding is smooth.

Whip cream; reserve 1 cup of whipped cream for garnish. Fold remainder into pudding. Line an 8½x4½x2½-inch loaf dish with waxed paper, extending paper beyond rim. Line bottom and sides with ladyfinger halves. Pour in half of the chocolate mixture. Add a layer of ladyfinger halves and the remaining pudding. Top with remaining ladyfinger halves.

Chill 3 to 4 hours or till firm. Lifting the waxed paper, remove charlotte russe from loaf dish and carefully transfer to serving plate; remove waxed paper. Garnish with the reserved whipped cream. Makes 6 servings.

**CHARTREUSE**—1. An aromatic liqueur. 2. An elaborate molded entrée.

The liqueur was first made in 1607 by Carthusian monks at Grenoble, France. The monks established another distillery in Tarragona, Spain, in 1903 when they were expelled from France.

The formula is still a secret. It is made on a brandy base with spices and herbs, including cinnamon, hyssop, and saffron. There are two types of chartreuse. One is a clear, light green color with a high alcoholic content. The other is yellow with a sweeter, less potent flavor.

Chartreuse can also refer to a molded entrée. This dish was originally made of root vegetables arranged in orderly rows, but later, meat, game, and poultry were included as ingredients. (See also *Liqueur*.)

**CHASSEUR** (*sha sûr'*)—A method of preparing food characterized by the addition of mushrooms as an ingredient or as a garnish. This method is sometimes used with small cuts of meat, poultry, or eggs. A sauce made in the chasseur manner is seasoned with wine and shallots. This may be called a hunter or chasseur sauce.

### Glamorous classic made from a mix

Garnish Chocolate Charlotte Russe with →
bunches of seedless, green grapes or whipped cream posies topped with candied cherries.

Arrange turkey slices filled with deviled ham in partially set consommé, then cover with more consommé, and chill until firm.

Cut serving of Chaud-Froid of Turkey using a 30-ounce size can with both ends removed. Bend can into oval for an interesting shape.

**CHÂTEAUBRIAND** *(shä tō brē än')*—A very thick, center cut from the beef tenderloin which is broiled or grilled. This classic was created by Montmireil, chef to French author and statesman, Châteaubriand.

Châteaubriand is usually served with a Béarnaise or château sauce. In restaurants, the menu generally lists it "for two."

## Châteaubriand

    1  1½- to 2-pound center-cut beef
          tenderloin
    2  tablespoons butter, melted
       Salt
       Béarnaise Sauce (See *Béarnaise*)

Place meat on rack of broiler pan. Brush with butter. Broil 4 inches from heat, 12 to 15 minutes; season with salt. Turn; brush again. Broil 12 to 15 minutes more; season second side. Outside will be browned and inside will be rare. Serve with Bearnaise Sauce. Serves 2.

**CHAUD-FROID** *(shō fräw')*—A dish consisting of poultry or game coated with aspic, jelly, or a sauce stiffened with gelatin. Sometimes meat, fish, seafood, tongue, or ham are substituted for the poultry. The translation from French means hot-cold, for the food is prepared hot and eaten cold.

Because of the advance preparation, decorative appearance, and ease in serving, chaud-froid is elegant for buffets.

## Chaud-Froid of Turkey

    12  thin slices from cooked boneless
           turkey roast
     2  4½-ounce cans deviled ham
    ½  cup finely chopped celery
     2  tablespoons finely chopped
           dill pickle
     4  teaspoons prepared horseradish
     2  envelopes (2 tablespoons)
           unflavored gelatin
     2  10½-ounce cans condensed
           consommé (gelatin added)
     2  chicken bouillon cubes
        Dash salt

If turkey slices are irregular in shape, trim to an oval about 3 inches at longest point. Mix deviled ham with celery, pickle, and horseradish; spread over 6 turkey slices. Top with remaining turkey slices making 6 "sandwiches."

Soften gelatin in 1 *can* consommé. Combine in a saucepan 2 cups water, bouillon cubes, and softened gelatin mixture; stir over low heat till bouillon and gelatin are dissolved. Add remaining consommé, dash salt, and 2 soup cans cold water. Chill till partially set.

Pour a little *more than half* of the partially set gelatin into 13x9x2-inch baking dish. Arrange the turkey sandwiches in the gelatin. Carefully pour remaining gelatin over sandwiches. Chill till firm. To serve, cut around turkey sandwiches, leaving a narrow border of gelatin on each. Garnish with ripe olives, deviled eggs, and lemon, if desired. Makes 6 servings.

**CHAYOTE** *(chī ō' tē)*—A green or white furrowed vegetable of the squash family. The pear-shaped chayote measures about three inches by eight inches and grows on a vine. Its soft seed is surrounded by a crystalline-textured flesh. The flavor is rather bland, resembling a cross between cucumber and zucchini. It is low in starch: about 30 calories per serving.

Chayote grows in tropical America, California and the southern United States. The Aztecs and Mayas were eating it before the Spaniards arrived in America.

When buying chayote, choose firm, young vegetables, avoiding any that are soft or wrinkled. Store in the refrigerator until ready to use. Cook as you would summer squash: steam, boil, fry, bake, or mix with other vegetables. Chayote holds its shape in cooking and is suitable for stuffing with meat mixtures. (See also *Squash.*)

**CHECKERBERRY** — The red fruit of the American wintergreen. It's also called winterberry. Checkerberries are used like cranberries in sauces, pies, puddings, or stuffings. (See also *Wintergreen.*)

**CHEDDAR**—A firm, ripened, natural cheese. The color ranges from white to a deep yellow. Flavor is rich and nutty.

Cheddar is named for the English village, Cheddar in Somersetshire, where it was first made during the sixteenth century or even earlier. The English brought their skill in making Cheddar to the American colonies where homemakers made it until commercial manufacturing took over the major part of the production.

***How Cheddar is produced:*** Whole milk from cows is used to make Cheddar. Federal law requires that cheese made with raw milk must be aged at least 60 days. Because Cheddar is aged six months to two years, raw or pasteurized milk can be used.

Ironically, the law prohibits importing Cheddar from its place of origin, England. Most Cheddar sold in America comes from New York, Wisconsin, and Vermont.

***Nutritional value:*** Cheddar supplies protein, fat, and minerals. One ounce of the cheese averages about 112 calories.

***Types of Cheddar:*** This popular cheese comes in a variety of flavors to please any taste. The natural unprocessed cheese ranges from very mild to very sharp while the pasteurized processed products are uniformly mild. Coon cheese is a well-cured Cheddar, and Colby is a soft, mild type of Cheddar. Monterey (or Jack) is a related type of semi-soft, ripened cheese.

***How to buy:*** In some stores, Cheddar is cut to order from a block. In this case, select cheese with a good bouquet, smooth texture, and a minimum of holes. Taste, if possible, to determine quality.

Most supermarkets stock prepackaged cheese cut in blocks or wedges, sliced, and shredded. It's impossible to see and taste this cheese before purchase. Experiment with brands and degrees of sharpness to find a personal favorite.

Peak-quality cheese will be selected from those aged from six to fourteen months. Good flavor is not bitter or soapy, and texture should be waxy, not rubbery.

***How to store:*** Cheddar should be stored in the refrigerator in its original wrapper. Once opened, cover with foil or clear plastic wrap to preserve its quality.

***How to use:*** A versatile cheese, Cheddar is eaten plain or used in many recipes. When served plain, it should be at room temperature. The sharp flavor and smooth texture complement fruit and crackers.

Cheddar may appear in any course at mealtime: it might be a main dish or sauce, or perhaps it could be a flavor accent to another food. (See also *Cheese.*)

Firm, tangy Cheddar is all-purpose.

# CHEESE

*A look at the development of cheese—natural and process—and its role in today's diet.*

Cheese is one of the oldest foods and one of the most nutritious foods known to man. An ancient legend credits the discovery of cheese to an Arab who was journeying across the desert, carrying his milk supply in a pouch made from a sheep's stomach. After many hours of travel, he stopped to satisfy his thirst. He found only a thin, watery liquid—most of the milk in the pouch had changed to a solid. Because of an intense hunger and thirst, he tasted the thick, white curd and found it delicious.

The change in the milk—magic to the Arab—is easily explained today. The combined action of the sun's heat and the sheep-stomach enzymes acting on the milk produced a curd. This reaction is used today as a basis for making cheese.

Historians won't hazard a guess about the discoverer of cheese, but they do believe it was developed shortly after the domestication of the cow, around 9000 B.C. One of the earliest written references to cheese occurs in the *Holy Bible,* when David is credited with having carried ten cheeses to Saul's camp at the time he encountered Goliath.

The ancient Greeks praised it as a gift from the God Aristaeus, protector of farmers and shepherds. They fed it to athletes who took part in the Olympic games. They also used cheese to reward children.

Cheese played such an important role in the Roman diet that special kitchens were built by the rich for making cheese. The lower classes had to cure their cheese in public smokehouses. The growth of the Roman empire spread the art of cheese-making over the continent.

During the Middle Ages, monks in European monasteries began making and improving the existing kinds of cheese. They developed more elaborate and complicated varieties, among them the soft-ripening cheeses for which France is famous. Their work was a turning point in the development of the art of cheesemaking.

Despite the wide popularity which accompanied the development of cheese, its acceptance declined during the Renaissance. Physicians wrote treatises denigrating its value; others attributed strange and suspicious powers to this once popular food. Superstitions linking eating cheese with illness were prevalent during the sixteenth and seventeenth centuries. During the eighteenth century, cheese was once again accepted—rising in popularity almost as quickly as it had fallen.

Fortunately for the New World, cheese accompanied the Pilgrims who settled in America, and with the arrival of cows from Europe, cheesemaking began. Prior to 1850, cheese production was entirely a home dairy operation. The first cheesemaking factory was built in Rome, New York, in 1851. Cheddar cheese was produced from milk supplied by nearby dairy farms. The development of other cheese factories soon spread along the eastern seaboard and westward to Wisconsin. Today, cheese is produced commercially in nearly every state, with Wisconsin and New York leading the nation's production.

The name of a cheese is often a clue to its history. Cheeses from Norway and Sweden often end with "ost," such as Gjetost and Kuminost. The more popular Danish

## Quick lunch for a blustery day

←Toasted Cheese Rolls are made with unsliced sandwich loaf and tangy cheese spread. Serve with hot cream of tomato soup.

cheeses have a common suffix, "bo," as in Molbo and Maribo. Many cheeses take their names from the town or area where they originated: Cheddar is an English village, Roquefort is a specific area in France, there's a Camembert in Normandy, Emmenthal or Emmenthaler (Swiss cheese) gets its name from the Emme valley in Switzerland, Parmesan is named for Parma in Italy, and Limburger comes from Limburg in Belgium.

Cheeses developed by the monks were often named after a saint, such as St. Claude and St. Benoit. Some cheeses are named for their appearance or the manner in which they are shaped. The rind of Pineapple cheese resembles the fruit. Brick cheese was originally formed with bricks, just as hand cheese was shaped by hand. Also, a cheese may be named for an ingredient, for example, sage cheese.

***How cheese is made:*** Although cow's milk is most often used in making cheese, milk from sheep, goats, buffalo, camels, reindeer, and other animals is used in other parts of the world. Cheesemaking involves separating milk into its liquid and solid components. This separation is achieved by adding either rennet (made from rennin, an enzyme found in the lining of a calf's stomach) or a special bacterial culture called a "starter."

Either rennet or starter, when added to milk, causes the milk to separate into white, soft lumps known as curd, and a thin, watery liquid called whey.

Different cultures and processes may affect the formation of the curd which, in turn, produces the differences found among the many varieties of cheese. A variation in temperature, moisture, or acidity influences the character of cheese.

After the curd is formed, it is cut or broken into smaller pieces. It may be cut into small cubes, or a special instrument called a cheese harp may be used to "comb" it into very long, thin strips. Once the curd is cut, it is drained to remove the whey, although for some cheeses the draining process is very slight.

Depending upon the cheese being produced, the curd may or may not be salted and pressed. Mold-ripened cheeses are either sprayed on the surface with mold, or they are inoculated with a mold culture to permit mold development throughout the cheese. Some cheeses are ripened under warm, moist conditions; others are ripened in cool, dry rooms. The rotation of the cheese during ripening and the length of time allowed for ripening also influence the texture of the cheese. Thus, at each step of the cheesemaking operation, a slight change in procedure is responsible for producing a different cheese.

Many kinds of cheese acquire their distinctive quality from a flavor additive. The type of mold used determines the characteristic flavors of Roquefort, Gorgonzola, Stilton, and Camembert. Hops are used to flavor German Hop cheese, while clover is used to make Sapsago. Some cheeses are wrapped in grape, fig, or chestnut leaves to absorb these delicate flavors as they ripen. Other cheeses are flavored with caraway seed, grape seed, saffron, hot peppers, cloves, or anise.

***Nutritional value:*** Approximately five quarts of milk are required to make one pound of Cheddar. Thus, Cheddar is a much more concentrated food. The protein content of cheese is about eight times greater than that found in an equal amount of milk; the fat content is about 20 to 30 percent of the total cheese weight.

The number of calories in different types of cheeses varies, but the most popular varieties in the United States market are whole milk cheeses which are very similar in fat and calorie content. In general, one ounce of cheese supplies about 100 calories. In addition, many of the vitamins and minerals normally found in milk—calcium, phosphorus, vitamin A—are present in cheese.

## Natural cheese

Cheese made directly from the curd of milk and not reprocessed or blended is known as natural cheese. Many of the natural cheeses are produced from unpasteurized milk. Cheeses are either unripened (uncured or fresh) or ripened (cured). Uncured or unripened cheeses include the normally quite bland cottage and cream

# KNOW YOUR CHEESE

1 Provolone (salami-style)
2 Longhorn
3 Midget Cheddar (sharp)
4 Gorgonzola
5 Parmesan
6 Edam
7 Cheddar (sharp)
8 Cheddar (soft)
9 Port du Salut
10 Provolone
11 Smoked Swiss
12 Cheddar (medium-sharp)
13 Swiss
14 Roquefort
15 Cheshire

16 Sapsago
17 Stilton
18 Gourmandise
19 Sharp Cheddar spread
20 Cheddar (sliced)
21 Pimiento cream-cheese dip
22 Bel Paese
23 Grape cheese
24 Bondost
25 Bondost with caraway
   seed
26 Christian IX (Danish
   spiced)
27 Herkimer (a cheddar type)
28 Sage

cheeses. Cured or ripened cheeses range in flavor from the mild Cheddar to the more pungent Limburger. If ripened, enzymes and microorganisms have been allowed to develop the flavor and texture characteristic of the particular kind of cheese. Length of ripening is often indicated on the package label as "mild," "mellow," "medium," "sharp," or "aged."

---

### Classification of natural cheese

The texture of different varieties of natural cheese is classified according to the manner in which it is ripened. In general, the softer the texture, the shorter the ripening period and the higher the moisture content. The blue-vein varieties are ripened with a mold culture which grows throughout the cheese, producing a characteristic flavor and appearance of the specific variety.

Unripened

| | | |
|---|---|---|
| Soft | Cottage, Cream, Neufchatel, Ricotta | |
| Firm | Gjetost, Mysost, Mozzarella | |

Ripened

| | |
|---|---|
| Soft | Brie, Camembert, Limburger |
| Semisoft | Bel Paese, Brick, Muenster, Port du Salut |
| Firm | Cheddar, Colby, Edam, Gouda, Provolone, Swiss |
| Very hard | Parmesan, Romano, Sapsago |
| Blue-vein | Blue, Gorgonzola, Roquefort, Stilton |

---

### A barbecue bonanza

←Grill-cooked vegetables such as Cheese-Topped Tomatoes and frozen broccoli spears add a fresh flavor to outdoor barbecuing.

Whey, which contains only a small amount of milk fat, is important in producing certain types of cheese. Mysost, Primost, and Gjetost, popular in Scandinavia, are examples of whey cheeses.

***How to select natural cheese:*** Domestic as well as imported cheeses are available in many American markets. However, many imported cheeses have been modified in production to comply with United States standards for cheese. Thus, many of the traditional cheeses made in Europe are available only for local consumption and cannot be imported into the United States.

The largest selection of cheeses is found generally in grocery store dairy counters, foreign food specialty stores, and cheese specialty stores. A cheese is best evaluated by its appearance, feel, smell, and taste. Many retailers offer samples to aid in selection. Knowing the characteristics of a particular variety is helpful.

Many natural cheeses are marketed in the shape unique to that kind: Gouda and Edam, for instance, are always flattened balls; other cheese varieties are characteristically sold in small blocks, wedges, or rounds. Oftentimes in specialty stores, a specific weight of cheese may be ordered, whereas in most local markets, much of the cheese is prepackaged.

***How to store natural cheese:*** The storage quality of cheese varies greatly. In general, the lower the moisture content the longer it may be stored. As a result, firm or very hard, ripened cheeses are less perishable than soft-ripened varieties.

Although the European connoisseur prefers a cool corner for storing cheese, the refrigerator provides the safest storage. Exposure to warm temperatures may cause cheese to "sweat" fat. Cheese should neither lose nor gain moisture—keep it well wrapped. Store blue-vein cheeses in a covered glass dish that allows air around the cheese, but not enough to dry it.

Some cheeses may be frozen although there is usually some loss of texture. To freeze, wrap pieces one-half pound or less in moisture-vaporproof wrap. Freeze cheese quickly at 0° or lower. To use, thaw in refrigerator in unopened package and serve as soon as possible after thawing. Cheeses that may be frozen include Brick, Camembert, Cheddar, Edam, Liederkranz, Mozzarella, Muenster, Parmesan, Port du Salut, Provolone, Romano, and Swiss. Soft cheeses are not recommended for freezing as they tend to separate after thawing.

***How to use natural cheese:*** For best flavor, most cheeses should be served slightly cooler than room temperature, so remove from refrigerator about one hour before serving. Remove soft cheeses, such as Camembert and Limburger, several hours before serving since they should be creamy when eaten. Serve fresh cheeses—cream, cottage, and Neufchatel—chilled.

Occasionally mold may appear on the outside of the cheese during storage in the refrigerator. This mold is not harmful. Simply cut it away and enjoy your cheese.

Natural cheeses are delicious as an appetizer, snack, sandwich, dessert, or as a part of the main dish. Fondue offers an excellent opportunity for serving cheese as a main dish. Try the dessert cheeses with wine and/or fresh fruit. Individual preference generally decides which cheese is served when. But there are over 400 varieties of cheese with which to experiment. Be adventurous and you'll enhance your cheese-eating pleasures.

Cheddar, Swiss, Gruyère, and Parmesan are often used in cooking. Be careful of too-high temperatures and prolonged cooking which causes natural-type cheeses to become leathery and stringy. Cheese requires no further cooking once it is melted. When possible, it should be added near the end of the cooking period. If shredded, grated, or cubed, less time is needed for melting the cheese.

# Process cheese

Much of the cheese manufactured and sold in the United States is pasteurized process cheese which is made from natural cheeses. Such cheeses include process cheese food, process cheese spread, cold-pack cheese, and cold-pack cheese food.

*Process cheese*—It is prepared by grinding and mixing together one or more natural cheeses with the aid of heat and an emulsifying agent. After blending and heating the cheeses, the mixture is poured into moisture-vaporproof containers. Pasteurization halts the action of enzymes and microorganisms; thus, no further ripening occurs. The emulsifier prevents fat separation during processing and helps produce an easy-to-slice cheese which melts readily when heated. The flavor of process cheese depends largely upon the natural cheese used. Pimientos, fruits, nuts, vegetables, meats, or smoke flavor may be added. Process cheese is packed in slices, loaves, and cut portions.

*Process cheese food*—while it is similar to process cheese, it is higher in moisture and slightly lower in milk fat content. It is prepared with less cheese and has milk, skim milk, or whey solids added. Pimientos, fruits, vegetables, bacon, or smoke flavor may be mixed in with the cheese. Milder in flavor, cheese food melts quicker than process cheese and is often used as a sandwich spread. It is available on the market in slices, rolls, links, and loaves.

*Process cheese spread*—it has more moisture and less milk fat than process cheese food. It is even easier to spread than cheese food and may contain the same flavoring ingredients as does process cheese. Process cheese spread is available packaged in jars or small loaves.

*Cold-pack cheese*—it is prepared by grinding and blending natural cheeses which have been well aged. Its flavor is similar to the natural cheeses used, and it is available in jars, rolls, and links.

*Cold-pack cheese food*—it differs from cold-pack cheese in that it includes skim milk or whey solids. Sweetening agents such as sugar and corn syrup may be added. Cold-pack cheese food may have a smoked flavor and/or contain pimientos, fruits, vegetables, and meats. It is higher in moisture than cold-pack cheese; thus, it is more easily spread. It is found in the local market in jars, rolls, and links.

***How to select process cheese:*** Reading the package label is of utmost importance when purchasing process cheese because of the wide variety of cheeses. The labels on pasteurized process cheese, cheese food, cheese spread, cold-pack cheese (sometimes called Club or Comminuted cheese), and cold-pack cheese food list the varieties of natural cheese used in making the product. Also listed are ingredients that have been added, as in the making of cheese food or cheese spread. Likewise, if a sharp or aged cheese is used, this is indicated.

***How to store process cheese:*** Like natural cheese, process cheese should be stored in the refrigerator. It has a high moisture content and must be wrapped tightly in moisture-vaporproof wrap to prevent drying on the surface of the cheese.

***How to use process cheese:*** Much of the popularity of process cheese is attributed to its relatively mild flavor and ease of use in cooking. For those who object to the more strongly flavored natural cheeses, process cheese offers many of the same flavors in a much milder form. The most popular process cheese, American, is made from natural Cheddar blended with similar varieties. Other process cheeses are made from Brick, Camembert, Gruyère, Limburger, and Swiss.

Unlike natural cheese, process cheese is not likely to string, to become rubbery, or to develop a grainy texture when heated. However, just as with natural cheese, low

To melt natural cheese, add to sauce over hot water. (Use water bath with chafing dish or double boiler.) Stir till melted.

temperatures and short-time cooking are recommended. A versatile food, process cheese lends itself to appetizers, snacks, sandwiches, fondues, and main dishes.

## Cheese Sauce

    2 tablespoons butter or margarine
    2 tablespoons all-purpose flour
    ¼ teaspoon salt
    1 cup milk
    4 ounces sharp natural Cheddar
       cheese, shredded (1 cup)

In saucepan melt butter; blend in flour and salt. Add milk, stirring constantly, till mixture thickens and bubbles. Remove from heat; add cheese. Stir to melt. Makes 1½ cups.

*Swiss-Cheddar Sauce:* Prepare Cheese Sauce *except* use 2 ounces sharp natural Cheddar cheese, shredded (½ cup) and 2 ounces Swiss cheese, shredded (½ cup). Makes 1½ cups.

*Blue Cheese Sauce:* Prepare Cheese Sauce *except substitute* 1 chicken bouillon cube, crumbled, for salt. *Omit* Cheddar cheese; add ¼ cup dairy sour cream and 1 ounce blue cheese, crumbled (¼ cup). Stir to melt. Heat through, *but do not boil.* Makes 1¼ cups.

## Swiss Cheese Sauce

    2 ounces process Swiss cheese,
       shredded (½ cup)
    ¼ cup mayonnaise or salad
       dressing
    ½ cup dairy sour cream
       Paprika

Combine cheese and mayonnaise. Cook over low heat, stirring constantly, till cheese melts. (If necessary, beat smooth with rotary beater.) Mix in sour cream; heat through *but do not boil.* Dash with paprika. Serve with hot cauliflower or cooked asparagus spears. Makes 1 cup.

## Jiffy Cheese Sauce

Combine one 10½-ounce can condensed cream of mushroom soup with ⅓ cup milk; heat. Add 4 ounces sharp process American cheese, shredded (1 cup). Stir to melt. Makes about 2½ cups.

## Rosy Cheese Fondue

    8 ounces sharp process American
       cheese, shredded (2 cups)
    2 ounces blue cheese, crumbled
       (½ cup)
    ½ cup condensed cream of tomato
       soup
    1 teaspoon Worcestershire sauce
    2 tablespoons dry sherry
       Toasted French bread cubes

In heavy saucepan combine first 4 ingredients. Cook and stir over low heat till smooth. Stir in wine. Transfer to fondue pot. Spear bread with fondue fork; dip in fondue. Makes 1 cup.

## Creamy Macaroni and Cheese Bake

Cook 2 cups elbow macaroni according to package directions; drain. Combine with ⅓ cup mayonnaise or salad dressing, ¼ cup chopped canned pimiento, ¼ cup chopped green pepper, and ¼ cup finely chopped onion.

    Blend together one 10½-ounce can condensed cream of mushroom soup, ½ cup milk, and 2 ounces sharp process American cheese, shredded (½ cup). Stir into macaroni; place in 1½-quart casserole. Top with additional 2 ounces sharp process American cheese, shredded (½ cup). Bake, uncovered, at 400° for 20 to 25 minutes. Makes 4 to 6 servings.

To melt process cheese, slice cheese directly into hot or cold sauce. Heat sauce only till cheese melts, stirring frequently.

## Cheese Soufflé

    ¼ cup butter or margarine
    ¼ cup all-purpose flour
    ½ teaspoon salt
       Dash cayenne
    1 cup milk
    8 ounces sharp process
       American cheese, thinly sliced
    4 eggs, separated

Melt butter; blend in flour, salt, and cayenne. Add milk all at once; cook over medium heat, stirring constantly, till mixture thickens and bubbles. Remove sauce from heat. Add thinly sliced cheese; stir till cheese melts.

    Beat egg yolks till very thick and lemon-colored. *Slowly* add cheese mixture, stirring constantly; cool slightly. Beat egg whites to stiff peaks. Gradually pour yolk mixture over egg whites; fold together. Pour into *ungreased* 1½-quart soufflé dish or casserole.

    For a top hat that puffs in the oven, trace a circle with spoon through mixture 1 inch from edge and 1 inch deep. Bake at 300° for 1¼ hours or till knife inserted off-center comes out clean. Immediately break apart into servings with 2 forks. Makes 4 servings.

## Cheese Ramekins

    3 ounces sharp process American
       cheese, shredded (¾ cup)
    2 slightly beaten egg yolks
    1 cup soft bread crumbs
    1 cup milk, scalded
    2 stiffly beaten egg whites

Reserve 2 tablespoons of the cheese. Combine remaining cheese, egg yolks, bread crumbs, and hot milk. Fold in egg whites. Turn into two 1½-cup casseroles. Top with reserved cheese. Bake at 325° for 35 to 40 minutes, or till knife inserted just off-center comes out clean. Serve immediately. Makes 2 servings.

### *Light as a feather*

Puffy Cheese Soufflé billows with top-hat →
appearance as it bakes in the oven. Delicate cheese flavor makes this a memorable dish.

## Cheese Fondue

1 clove garlic, halved
2 cups dry sauterne
¼ cup kirsch or dry sherry
1 teaspoon cornstarch
1½ pounds natural Swiss cheese, cut in thin strips (6 cups)
½ pound Gruyére cheese, shredded (2 cups)
¼ teaspoon ground nutmeg
French bread, cut in bite-size pieces, each with a crust

Rub inside of heavy saucepan with garlic. Pour in sauterne; warm till air bubbles rise and cover surface. (Don't cover or boil.) Blend kirsch *or* dry sherry with cornstarch; set mixture aside.

To warm sauterne, add handful of combined cheeses, stirring constantly. (Keep heat high but do not boil.) When melted, toss in another handful. After all cheese is blended and starting to bubble gently, stir in nutmeg, dash pepper, and kirsch mixture. Quickly transfer to fondue pot; keep warm. (If fondue becomes too thick, add a little *warm* sauterne.)

Spear bread on fork so crust is on outside. Swirl in fondue to coat. (Swirling keeps fondue stirred.) Makes 10 servings.

## Cheese Rabbit

2 11-ounce cans condensed Cheddar cheese soup
½ cup beer
¼ teaspoon Worcestershire sauce
Dash dry mustard
5 or 6 slices French bread, about ¾ inch thick, toasted
5 or 6 slices bacon, halved, crisp-cooked, and drained
5 or 6 thick tomato slices
1 3-ounce can mushroom crowns, drained (½ cup)

In saucepan combine soup, beer, Worcestershire sauce, and mustard. Stir to blend. Simmer over low heat 10 minutes, stirring frequently.

Place toasted bread slices in 13x9x2-inch baking dish. Top *each* with 2 pieces bacon, tomato slice, and 2 or 3 mushrooms. Pour sauce over all. Broil 3 to 4 inches from heat till cheese bubbles, about 3 minutes. Serves 5 or 6.

## Chicken-Cheese Chowder

4 slices bacon
¼ cup chopped onion
2 tablespoons chopped green pepper
2 cups milk
1 10½-ounce can condensed cream of chicken soup
1 cup diced cooked chicken
2 tablespoons chopped canned pimiento
Dash salt
4 ounces Monterey Jack cheese, shredded (1 cup)
Dash paprika *or* ground mace

Cook bacon till crisp; drain, reserving drippings. Crumble bacon. Put 2 tablespoons reserved drippings in saucepan. Add onion and green pepper; cook till tender. Add milk, soup, chicken, pimiento, salt, and *half* the bacon. Heat through. Add cheese; stir to melt. To serve, garnish with remaining bacon and paprika *or* mace. Makes 4 or 5 servings.

## Canadian Cheese Soup

½ cup finely chopped onion
¼ cup butter or margarine
½ cup all-purpose flour
4 cups milk
4 cups chicken broth
½ cup finely diced carrot
½ cup finely diced celery
Dash *each* salt and paprika
4 ounces sharp process American cheese, shredded (1 cup)

Cook onion in butter till tender but not brown. Blend in flour. Add milk, chicken broth, carrot, celery, salt, and paprika. Cook over medium heat, stirring constantly, till mixture thickens and bubbles. Reduce heat. Add cheese; stir to melt. Simmer 15 minutes. Garnish with popcorn, if desired. Makes 8 servings.

### *Soups to savor*

Creamy Chicken-Cheese Chowder studded →
with bacon *or* golden Canadian Cheese Soup
fulfill the bill for a late-evening supper.

## Toasted Cheese Rolls

Cut crusts from top and sides of 1 unsliced sandwich loaf, about 11 inches long. Make 8 slices crosswise, *cutting to, but not through* bottom crust; make one cut lengthwise down center of loaf. Place on baking sheet.

Blend ½ cup butter or margarine, softened, with two 5-ounce jars sharp process cheese spread. Spread mixture between slices, over top, and sides. Sprinkle lightly with poppy seed *or* celery seed. Tie string around loaf to hold together. Bake at 400° about 15 minutes, or till cheese melts and bread is crusty. Serve hot like pan rolls with soup or salad. Makes 16.

## Cheese Crescents

Prepare 2 cups packaged biscuit mix according to package directions. Knead 8 to 10 times. Roll out on floured surface to 14-inch circle.

Brush with 2 tablespoons butter, melted; sprinkle with 4 ounces sharp natural Cheddar cheese, shredded (1 cup). Cut in 10 wedges. Starting at wide end, roll each to form crescent. Put crescents, point down, on lightly greased baking sheet. Bake at 450° for 10 minutes or till brown. Serve hot. Makes 10.

## Airy Cheese Rolls

  1 package active dry yeast
1¾ cups milk, scalded
  4 ounces sharp process American
     cheese, shredded (1 cup)
 ¼ cup sugar
  2 tablespoons shortening
  4 cups sifted all-purpose flour
  1 beaten egg
 ½ cup cornmeal

Soften yeast in ¼ cup *warm* water. In large bowl of electric mixer combine hot milk, next 3 ingredients, and 1 teaspoon salt. Stir till cheese melts; cool to lukewarm. Add *2 cups* of the flour; beat 2 minutes at medium speed.

Add egg, yeast, cornmeal, and remaining flour. Beat 2 minutes. Cover; let rise in warm place till double, about 1¼ hours; stir down.

Fill greased 2½-inch muffin pans ½ full. Cover; let rise till double, about 45 minutes. Bake at 375° for 15 to 20 minutes. Makes 24.

## Cheese-Topped Tomatoes

  5 large tomatoes
 ¼ cup soft bread crumbs
 ¼ cup shredded sharp process
     American cheese
  1 tablespoon butter, melted
     Snipped parsley

Slice off tops of tomatoes. Cut zigzag edges; season with salt and pepper. Combine crumbs, cheese, and butter; sprinkle over tomatoes. Garnish with parsley. Heat tomatoes on foil over *hot* coals (or bake at 375°) till warmed through. Serve immediately. Makes 5 servings.

## Three-Cheese Mold

Mix 1½ teaspoons unflavored gelatin with ¼ cup cold water; heat till dissolved. Beat together 2 ounces blue cheese, crumbled (½ cup); 2 ounces natural Cheddar cheese, shredded (½ cup); and ½ cup cream-style cottage cheese.

Beat in ¼ cup dairy sour cream, 1½ teaspoons grated onion, ½ teaspoon Worcestershire sauce, and dissolved gelatin. Pour into 2-cup mold. Chill till firm. Serve with crackers.

Open the party with creamy Three-Cheese Mold, a do-ahead appetizer made with a trio of cheeses—blue, Cheddar, and cottage.

**CHEESECAKE**—A rich, creamy dessert prepared from unripened cheese combined with milk, eggs, and flavorings. Sometimes fruit juice or rind and/or nuts are added. Some are baked, others are chilled. Cheesecake has a velvety-smooth texture and is often served, topped with fresh fruit.

Making and serving cheesecake dates back to ancient times. Greeks and Romans featured it as a festival food. Essays were written on the merits of one kind of cheesecake over another. In the United States, cheesecake was so well liked by George Washington that Mrs. Washington included recipes in her cook book.

The cheese used in making this rich dessert varies from cream-style to dry-curd cottage, farmer's, pot or cream cheese. Today's cheesecakes are often made with a crumb crust on the bottom and part way up the sides. For this type of cake, a springform pan is best. When the sides of the pan are removed, the cheesecake stands ready for cutting.

Cheesecake may also be made in a pie plate—thus the name cheesecake pie. The crust may vary from a standard pastry to a crumb crust or puff pastry.

## Speedy Cheesecake Pie

    1 cup graham cracker crumbs
    3 tablespoons butter, melted
    1 8-ounce package cream cheese,
      softened
    ½ cup sugar
    1 tablespoon lemon juice
    ½ teaspoon vanilla
    2 eggs
    1 cup dairy sour cream
    2 tablespoons sugar
    ½ teaspoon vanilla

Combine crumbs and butter. Press into buttered 8-inch pie plate, building up sides. Meanwhile, beat cream cheese till fluffy; blend in ½ cup sugar, lemon juice, ½ teaspoon vanilla, and dash salt. Add eggs, one at a time, beating well after each. Pour into crust. Bake at 325° for 30 minutes. Combine dairy sour cream, sugar, and vanilla; spoon over top of pie. Bake 10 minutes more. Cool. Chill several hours. Serve with fresh or frozen fruit, if desired.

## Angel Cheesecake

*A favorite when entertaining guests—*

**Crust:**
    1 cup crushed zwieback
      (about 9 slices)
    2 tablespoons sugar
    2 tablespoons butter or margarine,
      melted
**Filling:**
    ½ cup sugar
    2 8-ounce packages cream cheese,
      softened
    1 teaspoon vanilla
    ¼ teaspoon salt
    ½ teaspoon grated lemon peel
    2 cups dairy sour cream
    5 egg yolks
    5 egg whites
    1 tablespoon lemon juice
    ½ cup sugar
**Cherry Sauce:**
    ½ cup sugar
    2 tablespoons cornstarch
    Dash salt
    1 20-ounce can frozen, pitted,
      tart red cherries (with syrup),
      thawed

*Crust:* Mix zwieback crumbs, 2 tablespoons sugar, and butter or margarine; press on bottom of *ungreased* 9-inch springform pan.

*Filling:* Gradually beat ½ cup sugar into softened cream cheese. Beat in vanilla, ¼ teaspoon salt, and grated lemon peel. Add sour cream and blend in egg yolks.

Beat egg whites with lemon juice to soft peaks; gradually add ½ cup sugar, beating till *very stiff,* but not dry, peaks form. Fold cheese mixture into egg whites. Pour into crumb-lined pan. Bake at 325° for 1¼ hours or till knife inserted off-center comes out clean.

Cool 10 minutes; run spatula around edge of top. (Cake settles slightly as it cools—loosening edge lets it do this evenly.) Cool thoroughly, about 1½ hours, before removing sides of pan. Chill thoroughly in refrigerator.

Pass *Cherry Sauce:* In saucepan combine ½ cup sugar, cornstarch, and dash salt. Stir in thawed cherries with syrup. Cook and stir over medium heat till mixture thickens and bubbles. Reduce heat; simmer 10 minutes. Chill before serving. Makes 10 servings.

## Strawberry-Glazed Cheesecake

**Crust:**
- 1¾ cups fine graham-cracker crumbs (about 20 crackers)
- ¼ cup finely chopped walnuts
- ½ teaspoon ground cinnamon
- ½ cup butter or margarine, melted

**Filling:**
- 3 well-beaten eggs
- 2 8-ounce packages cream cheese, softened
- 1 cup sugar
- 2 teaspoons vanilla
- ½ teaspoon almond extract
- ¼ teaspoon salt
- 3 cups dairy sour cream

**Glaze:**
- 2 cups fresh strawberries
- ¾ cup water

. . .

- 2 tablespoons cornstarch
- ½ cup sugar
- Red food coloring

*Crust:* In bowl combine graham-cracker crumbs, walnuts, and cinnamon. Add melted butter or margarine; mix thoroughly. Press on bottom and sides of 9-inch springform pan. Sides should be about 1¾ inches high.

*Filling:* Combine eggs, cream cheese, ½ cup sugar, vanilla, almond extract, and salt; beat till smooth. Blend in sour cream. Pour into crumb crust. Bake at 375° about 35 minutes or just till set. Cool. Chill thoroughly, about 4 to 5 hours. (Filling will be soft.)

*Glaze:* Crush *1 cup* of the strawberries. Add water and cook 2 minutes; sieve. Mix cornstarch with ½ cup sugar; slowly stir in hot berry mixture. Bring to boiling, stirring constantly. Cook and stir till mixture is thick and clear. (Add a few drops red food coloring, if desired.) Cool to room temperature. Halve remaining strawberries. Place atop chilled cheesecake; pour strawberry glaze over. Chill about 2 hours. Makes 10 servings.

### Cheesecake at its best

← Luscious Strawberry-Glazed Cheesecake—a winner at any table. In the summer, use fresh raspberries or blueberries for glaze.

For Cheesecake Supreme, pat dough on sides of springform pan. Rotate pan on edge to insure uniform thickness of crust.

## Cheesecake Supreme

**Crust:**
- 1 cup sifted all-purpose flour
- ¼ cup sugar
- 1 teaspoon grated lemon peel

. . .

- ½ cup butter or margarine
- 1 slightly beaten egg yolk
- ¼ teaspoon vanilla

**Filling:**
- 5 8-ounce packages cream cheese, softened
- ¼ teaspoon vanilla
- ¾ teaspoon grated lemon peel
- 1¾ cups sugar
- 3 tablespoons all-purpose flour
- 4 or 5 eggs (1 cup)
- 2 egg yolks
- ¼ cup whipping cream

*Crust:* Mix first 3 ingredients. Cut in butter till crumbly. Add 1 beaten egg yolk and ¼ teaspoon vanilla; mix well. Pat ⅓ of the dough on bottom of 9-inch springform pan *with sides removed*. Bake at 400° for 8 minutes; cool. Butter sides of pan; attach to bottom. Pat remaining dough on sides 1¾ inches high.

*Filling:* Beat cheese; add ¼ teaspoon vanilla and ¾ teaspoon lemon peel. Mix 1¾ cups sugar, 3 tablespoons flour, and ¼ teaspoon salt; slowly add to cheese. Add eggs and 2 egg yolks, one at a time, beating well after each addition. Gently stir in whipping cream. Turn into pan. Bake at 450° for 12 minutes; reduce heat to 300°. Bake 55 minutes longer or till knife inserted off-center comes out clean. Cool 30 minutes; loosen sides of pan. Cool 30 minutes more; remove pan sides. Cool 2 hours; chill. Serves 12.

**CHEESE STRAW**—A long, narrow piece of pastry or dough flavored with cheese. The cheese may be incorporated into the dough or sprinkled on top of the dough. These tidbits are served as accompaniments to soups and salads or as appetizers.

## Peanut-Cheese Straws

⅓ cup milk
1 tablespoon sugar
½ teaspoon salt
2 tablespoons butter or margarine
·  ·  ·
¼ cup warm water
1 package active dry yeast
1 well-beaten egg
1¾ to 2 cups sifted all-purpose
    flour
·  ·  ·
¼ cup butter or margarine
3 ounces sharp Cheddar cheese,
    shredded (¾ cup)
½ cup chopped dry roasted peanuts
1 tablespoon water

Scald milk. Stir in sugar, salt, and 2 tablespoons butter; cool to lukewarm.

Measure warm water into mixing bowl. Sprinkle in yeast; stir till dissolved. Stir in lukewarm milk mixture. Setting aside 1 tablespoon of the beaten egg, stir in remaining egg and *half* the flour. Beat about 2 minutes at medium speed on electric mixer. Stir in enough additional flour to make a soft dough. Turn out onto lightly floured surface.

Knead till smooth and elastic, about 5 minutes. Place in greased bowl, turning to grease top of dough. Cover; let rise in warm place till double, about 30 minutes. Punch dough down and turn out onto floured surface. Roll out to a 10x6-inch rectangle, about ¼ inch thick. Dot center third with *2 tablespoons* of the remaining butter cut in small pieces, and sprinkle with *half* the shredded cheese. Fold one end of dough over to cover cheese. Dot with second 2 tablespoons butter and sprinkle with remaining cheese; fold last third of dough over to cover this cheese-butter layer.

Press edges of dough together firmly. Cover; let rest 20 minutes. Sprinkle board with *half* of the chopped nuts. Roll dough out over nuts into a 11x6-inch rectangle.

Combine reserved egg and 1 tablespoon water; brush over dough and sprinkle with remaining ¼ cup nuts. Cut dough in strips 6 inches long and ½ inch wide. Using spatula, place on greased baking sheet, about ½ inch apart. Let rise, uncovered, in a warm place, about 30 minutes. Bake at 400° till golden, about 10 to 12 minutes. Makes 2 dozen.

**CHERIMOYA** (*cher' uh moi' uh*)—A fancy, tropical fruit with a soft, custardlike center. It is heart-shaped, and the skin is green when the fruit is ripe. The seeds are not eaten. It is grown in Hawaii, California and Florida and is sometimes identified as a custard apple. (See also *Fruit*.)

**CHERRIES JUBILEE**—The name given to a glamorous dessert made using dark, sweet cherries flamed with brandy and spooned over ice cream. For a dramatic effect, dim the lights in the room just before lighting the brandy with a match.

## Cherries Jubilee

Drain one 16-ounce can pitted dark sweet cherries (2 cups), reserving syrup. In saucepan blend ¼ cup sugar and 2 tablespoons cornstarch. Gradually stir in reserved cherry syrup, mixing well. Cook and stir over medium heat till mixture thickens and bubbles. Remove from heat and stir in cherries.

Turn cherry mixture into heat-proof bowl or top pan (blazer) of chafing dish. (Be sure bottom pan of chafing dish is filled with hot water; keep hot over flame.)

Heat ¼ cup brandy, kirsch, *or* cherry brandy in small metal pan with long handle. If desired, heated brandy can be poured into a large ladle. Carefully ignite heated brandy and pour over cherry mixture. Stir to blend brandy into sauce. Serve immediately over scoops of vanilla ice cream. Makes 2 cups sauce.

### *A dramatic ending to the meal*

Cherries Jubilee, a gourmet dessert, makes→ even the beginning cook in the kitchen turn into a cook-at-the-table showman.

**CHERRY**—A small, round or heart-shaped fruit having a single, smooth pit or stone belonging to the genus *Prunus*. The fruit is divided into two types—the sweet cherries and the sour or tart cherries, and both are related to the stone-fruit group that includes peaches, apricots, and plums.

It is surmised that cherry trees were first cultivated in China several thousand years ago; however, there is no proof of this. Records of cherries in Italy around 69 B.C. have been found.

Some authorities believe that the sweet cherry originated in the Caspian and Black Sea areas, and that birds may have carried the seeds of the sweet cherry tree from Asia, spreading the fruit over the European continent.

Cherries were brought to America by early settlers, and there are records of cherry trees having been here by 1629. Of course, the legend of George Washington and his cherry tree during the colonial period is familiar to all. Later, around the mid-1800's, the cherry industry got its start on the West Coast.

*Nutritional value:* Cherries are moderate in calorie yield. For the sour ones, about ½ cup raw cherries has 58 calories; ½ cup canned (water pack) has 43 calories; and ½ cup canned in syrup has 89 calories. For sweet cherries, 15 large ones have 70 calories, and ½ cup canned in syrup yields 89 calories. Cherries contain some vitamin A and some B vitamins.

*Kinds of cherries:* The most popular sweet cherries are the large, dark red Bing; the Lambert, a dark red cherry; the Tartarian, a small, purplish black cherry; and the Chapman, a large, round cherry. The favored light-colored sweet cherry is called the Napoleon or Royal Ann. This cherry has a light golden color with a red blush over it. It's used mainly for canning and is rarely found as a fresh fruit.

Of the sour cherries, the Montmorency is probably the most widely used variety in the United States. Other sour cherries include the English Morello and the Early Richmond. Most of the sour cherries are either canned or used cooked, while sweet cherries are usually eaten fresh.

Both types of cherries grow best where the temperatures are not extreme—neither too hot nor too cold. The spring blossoms are very susceptible to frost. Sour cherries, however, are a little more hardy than the sweet variety. Major areas of production for the sour cherries are in New York and the areas around the Great Lakes, mainly in Michigan and Wisconsin. Sweet cherry varieties come mainly from California, Oregon, and Washington.

The season for sweet cherries is from May to August, while the season for sour cherries is shorter, usually June and July.

*How to select:* Buy cherries that are fresh, firm, bright, and a good color for the particular variety. For most varieties of sweet cherries, a very dark color is a good indication of maturity. They should be glossy and have fresh stems. Cherries that are not ripe will be hard, will lack juiciness, and often have an acid taste. Overripe cherries will be soft, shriveled, dull in appearance, and may be leaking juice.

Cherries can be purchased year-round as canned and frozen products. Usually, the sour cherries will be pitted, while the sweet cherries can be purchased both pitted or unpitted. Ready-to-use cherry pie filling, candied cherries, cherry jams and preserves, and red or green maraschino cherries are grocery shelf staples.

*How to store:* After purchasing cherries, sort through them and discard any undesirable ones. Handle lightly as cherries are delicate and bruise easily. Refrigerate in plastic bags and use as soon as possible. Be sure to rinse them before using.

Cherries may be canned at home by either the cold-pack or hot-pack methods; they also freeze well. Sour cherries may be frozen in either a syrup or a sugar pack. To syrup-pack sour cherries, remove

### Cherries used many luscious ways

Beginning at top of page is Cherry Meringue Cake, Cherry Bavarian, Creamy Cherry Pie, Cherry Dessert Salad, Molded Cherry Ring, and Cherry Shortcake Towers.

stems, wash, drain, and pit. Pack the cherries into freezer containers and cover the cherries with a cold, very heavy or extra heavy syrup, depending on the tartness of the fruit. Be sure to leave headspace; then seal, label, and freeze. To sugar-pack sour cherries, stem, wash, drain, and pit them. To each quart of fruit add ¾ cup sugar and mix lightly until the sugar is dissolved. Pack into freezer container—leave headspace. Seal, label, and freeze.

Sweet cherries can be syrup-packed. Stem, wash, drain, and pit them, if desired. Add ½ teaspoon ascorbic acid color keeper to each quart medium syrup. Pack the fruit into containers and cover it with syrup, leaving a headspace. Seal, label with contents and date, then freeze.

**How to use:** Sweet cherries are usually eaten fresh, but they also make delightful additions to fresh fruit salads and desserts. Cherries Jubilee is an excellent example of canned sweet cherries at their best. They are also delicious in sauces spooned over cake or in molded salads and desserts.

## Cherry Bavarian

*A two-layer beauty made in two separate molds—*

>    ¾ cup sugar
>    2 envelopes unflavored gelatin
>        (2 tablespoons)
>    ¼ teaspoon salt
>   1½ cups milk
>    3 beaten egg yolks
>    1 3-ounce package cream cheese, cut
>        up and softened
>   1½ cups light cream
>    ½ teaspoon vanilla
>    ½ teaspoon almond extract
>    3 stiffly beaten egg whites
>            • • •
>    1 16-ounce can pitted dark
>        sweet cherries
>    1 3-ounce package cherry-flavored
>        gelatin
>    ½ cup whipping cream

*Creamy Layer:* In saucepan combine sugar, unflavored gelatin, and salt. Stir in milk, then yolks. Cook and stir till thickened slightly.

With rotary beater, beat egg mixture into softened cream cheese until smooth. Add light cream, vanilla, and almond extract. Chill till gelatin mixture is partially set. Gently fold in stiffly beaten egg whites. Pour into 5-cup mold. Chill till firm, about 8 hours or overnight.

*Cherry Layer:* Drain cherries, reserving syrup. Cut up cherries. Add water to reserved syrup to make 1¾ cups. In saucepan combine syrup and cherry-flavored gelatin. Heat, stirring constantly, till gelatin dissolves. Chill till slightly thickened. Whip cream; fold into thickened cherry gelatin along with drained cherries. Pour into 3½-cup mold. Chill overnight. To serve, carefully unmold on top of Creamy Layer. Makes 8 to 10 servings.

Its attractive red color and ease of preparation makes canned cherry pie filling a good item to keep on the emergency shelf. In addition to using it in pies, it can be used in salads, desserts, or heated and served with cooked ham for the entrée.

## Cherry Dessert Salad

In saucepan blend ⅓ cup sugar and 1 envelope unflavored gelatin (1 tablespoon). Stir in 1 cup unsweetened pineapple juice; heat and stir till gelatin is dissolved. Remove from heat. Beat into one 3-ounce package softened cream cheese till smooth. Add ¾ cup unsweetened pineapple juice and 1 tablespoon lemon juice. Chill till partially set. Whip till fluffy. Prepare one 2-ounce envelope dessert topping mix according to package directions. Fold into gelatin. Pour into 6½-cup mold. Chill till *almost* firm.

In small saucepan combine one 3-ounce package cherry-flavored gelatin and ¾ cup water. Heat till gelatin dissolves. Add one 21-ounce can cherry pie filling. Stir well. Chill till partially set, stirring occasionally. Spoon over cream cheese layer. Chill till the gelatin mixture is firm, about 6 hours or overnight.

Unmold and serve with *Custard Sauce:* In heavy saucepan mix 2 beaten eggs, dash salt, and ¼ cup sugar. Gradually stir in 2 cups milk, scalded and slightly cooled. Cook over low heat, stirring constantly, till mixture coats a metal spoon. Remove from heat. Cool pan at once in cold water; stir 1 or 2 minutes. Add 1 teaspoon vanilla. Chill. Makes 8 servings.

## Cherry Meringue Cake

1 package 1-layer-size white cake
    mix
¾ teaspoon rum extract

• • •

1 21-ounce can cherry pie filling
3 egg whites
½ teaspoon vanilla
¼ teaspoon cream of tartar
6 tablespoons sugar

Prepare cake following package directions adding rum flavoring to batter. Turn into a greased and floured 9x9x2-inch baking pan. Bake according to package directions. Cool.

Top with cherry pie filling. Beat egg whites with vanilla and cream of tartar till soft peaks form. Gradually add sugar, beating till stiff peaks form. Spread meringue over cherry filling, sealing to edges all around. Bake at 350° till peaks are golden brown, about 20 to 25 minutes. Trim with maraschino cherries, if desired. Makes 9 servings.

## Cherry Parfaits

*Layers of instant pudding, cherry pie filling, and almonds alternate in this luscious dessert—*

1 cup milk
1 cup dairy sour cream
¼ teaspoon almond extract
1 3⅝- *or* 3¾-ounce package
    *instant* vanilla pudding mix

• • •

1 21-ounce can cherry pie filling
    Toasted slivered almonds

In mixing bowl combine milk, sour cream, and almond extract. Add pudding mix and beat with rotary beater till creamy and well blended, about 2 minutes. Fill parfait glasses with alternate layers of pudding, cherry pie filling, and almonds; chill. Garnish with additional almonds. Makes 6 servings.

When sweetened, sour cherries are delicious in pies or shortcakes. They can be used in low-calorie salads. (See *Bing Cherry, Fruit, Maraschino Cherry, Montmorency Cherry* for additional information.)

## Cherry Shortcake Towers

In mixing bowl sift together 2 cups sifted all-purpose flour, 1 tablespoon sugar, 4 teaspoons baking powder, and ½ teaspoon salt. Cut in ½ cup butter or margarine till mixture resembles coarse crumbs. Combine 1 beaten egg and ⅔ cup milk; add all at once to dry ingredients, stirring just to moisten.

Turn dough out onto floured surface. Knead gently about 30 seconds. Pat or roll dough to ½-inch thickness. Cut out 9 biscuits with floured 2½-inch cutter.

Bake on *ungreased* baking sheet at 450° for 8 to 10 minutes. Split shortcakes in half. Using three halves for each tower, fill and top with Cherry Topping. Garnish with whipped cream. Serve warm. Makes 6 servings.

*Cherry Topping:* In saucepan combine ⅓ cup sugar, 2 tablespoons cornstarch, and dash salt. Drain one 20-ounce can pitted tart red cherries (water pack), reserving juice. Add water to juice to make 1¼ cups liquid. Gradually stir cherry juice into sugar mixture; cook and stir till thickened and bubbly. Cook 1 minute more. Remove from heat. Add 1 tablespoon butter, drained cherries, 6 to 8 drops almond extract, 6 to 8 drops vanilla, and ¼ teaspoon red food coloring. Cool.

## Molded Cherry Ring

*A delicious, low calorie salad—*

Drain one 20-ounce can pitted tart red cherries (water pack), reserving juice. Add enough water to juice to make 3 cups. In saucepan soften 2 envelopes unflavored gelatin (2 tablespoons) in juice mixture. Cook and stir over medium heat till gelatin is dissolved. Add non-caloric sweetener to equal ¾ cup sugar, 5 drops red food coloring, and drained cherries; bring the cherry mixture just to boiling.

Remove from heat; add ½ cup lemon juice. Chill till partially set, stirring occasionally. Fold in ¼ cup chopped celery, if desired. Turn into 5½-cup ring mold. Chill till firm.

Serve with *Fluffy Whipped Topping:* Pour ⅓ cup evaporated *skim* milk into mixing bowl. Chill the bowl and beaters. Add 1 tablespoon sugar and ¼ teaspoon vanilla. Whip with rotary beater or electric mixer to stiff peaks. *Use immediately.* Serves 8 or 9.

Who could resist a wedge of this tart, yet sweet Red Cherry Pie. The filling is an uncooked mixture of canned tart red cherries and can be ready by the time the pastry is rolled out.

## Red Cherry Pie

    ¾ cup juice from cherries
    3 cups canned pitted tart red
        cherries (water pack)
    1 cup sugar
    2 tablespoons quick-cooking
        tapioca
   10 drops red food coloring
    3 to 4 drops almond extract
      Pastry for 9-inch lattice top
        pie (See *Pastry*)
    1 tablespoon butter or margarine

Combine juice from cherries, cherries, sugar, tapioca, food coloring, almond extract, and dash salt. Let stand 20 minutes.

Line 9-inch pie plate with pastry. Fill with cherry mixture. Dot with butter or margarine. Adjust lattice crust atop pie. Crimp edge high. Bake at 400° till crust is lightly browned, about 50 to 55 minutes.

## Creamy Cherry Pie

*Perfect for the February holidays—*

Drain one 20-ounce can pitted tart red cherries (water pack), reserving ¾ cup juice. In saucepan mix together ⅔ cup sugar, ¼ cup cornstarch, and ¼ teaspoon salt. Gradually blend in reserved juice and ¼ cup water. Cook and stir till mixture thickens and bubbles. Remove from heat. Stir in ¼ teaspoon red food coloring, ¼ teaspoon almond extract, and drained cherries. Cool slightly.

Prepare one 9-inch pastry shell (See *Pastry*), crimping edges high. Bake. Reserving ¼ cup cherry mixture for garnish if desired, pour remaining cherries into the baked shell.

Prepare one 3⅝- or 3¾-ounce package *instant* vanilla pudding mix according to package directions *using only 1½ cups milk*. Let stand 1 to 2 minutes. Spoon over cherry filling. Chill. Garnish with reserved cherries.

## Fresh Cherry Pie

> Pastry for 8-inch lattice-top
>   pie (See *Pastry*)
> 3 cups pitted fresh ripe tart red
>   cherries
> 1 to 1½ cups sugar
> ¼ cup all-purpose flour
> 2 tablespoons butter or margarine

Line 8-inch pie plate with pastry. Combine cherries, sugar, flour, and dash salt. Turn into pastry-lined pie plate. Dot with butter or margarine. Adjust lattice top; seal. Bake at 400° for 50 to 55 minutes.

**CHERRY TOMATO**—A variety of tomato that is about the size and shape of a cherry and bright red in color. It usually ranges in size from 1 to 1½ inches but it may grow as large as 2 inches. It is sometimes available with its green calyx intact.

Cherry tomatoes add interesting color and shape contrasts to salads and vegetable platters. They make excellent hors d'oeuvres for eating as is or with a well-seasoned dip. (See also *Tomato*.)

**CHERVIL** *(chŭr' vil)*—A delicate herb, related to the parsley family, with a light green, lacy, fernlike leaf. Chervil has a light, aromatic flavor, which some identify as faintly aniselike.

It is combined with more robust herbs in the familiar bouquet garni and is also an ingredient in fines herbes.

By itself, chervil is especially delicious in egg or cheese dishes and makes an attractive and pleasing garnish for buttered carrots. It is also a good addition to soups, salads, and stews.

In the United States chervil is grown commercially and can be found in many herb gardens. Chervil can also be purchased as dried leaves. (See also *Herb*.)

**CHESS PIE**—The name given to a rich, buttery, sugary, custard-type pie containing a bit of lemon juice added for flavor. The filling sometimes includes raisins and nuts and is baked in a rich pastry shell. This delightful dessert is an old-fashioned Southern favorite. (See also *Pie*.)

## Chess Pie

*Small pieces of this pie are usually served—*

Cream ½ cup butter and 2 cups sugar. Beat in 1 tablespoon all-purpose flour and 1 tablespoon yellow cornmeal. Add 5 well-beaten eggs, 1 cup milk, 2 tablespoons lemon juice, and 1 teaspoon vanilla; beat. Pour into 1 unbaked Rich Pastry Shell. Bake at 350° till knife inserted in center of pie comes out clean, about 55 minutes.

*Rich Pastry Shell:* Sift together 1 cup sifted all-purpose flour, ¼ teaspoon salt, and ¼ teaspoon baking powder. Cut in 6 tablespoons butter till size of small peas.

Gradually add 3 to 4 tablespoons milk, mixing till dough can be formed into a ball. Roll out and fit into 9-inch pie plate (have pastry edges crimped high because filling is generous).

**CHESTNUT**—A sweet nut that grows in a prickly burr. Since a blight destroyed many chestnut trees in America several decades ago, most chestnuts found in the markets are imported from Italy.

Chestnuts are cooked before eating, usually by roasting or boiling. They can be eaten plain or used in other mixtures.

To roast fresh chestnuts: with a sharp knife, make cross-slits on the flat side of each chestnut. Place in a shallow baking pan and roast at 400° for 15 minutes, tossing occasionally. Serve piping hot.

To boil fresh chestnuts: with a sharp knife, slash the flat side of each chestnut. Place in a saucepan of cold water. Bring to boiling; boil 8 to 10 minutes. Remove from heat. With slotted spoon remove 3 or 4 chestnuts at a time from water. Peel off the outer shells and the brown inner skins, taking care to keep the chestnuts whole. For ease in peeling, leave unpeeled chestnuts in warm cooking water till peeled.

Chestnuts can also be purchased in cans, either whole or puréed. Puréed or chopped, cooked chestnuts make a delicious addition to poultry stuffing. Preserved chestnuts are also available, either whole nuts or in pieces. Preserved marrons, called *marrons glacés*, are large, special chestnuts candied in France. These are delicious confections. (See also *Nut*.)

# CHICKEN

*Ideas for using this international favorite
ranging from simple soups to exotic entrées.*

The sweet, delicately flavored flesh of this domesticated fowl is a most versatile food. Chicken is tasty enough to be enjoyed eaten alone, yet delicate enough to blend well with so many other foods that it can be eaten often without becoming boring. Because of its flavor and digestibility, chicken is a favorite with all ages.

Today's chickens descended from fowl that were cackling in the jungles of southwestern Asia thousands of years ago. The first time our ancestors had the ingenious idea of using them for food was about 1400 B.C. Since then, man has domesticated the bird and chicken raising has spread extensively. Spanish explorers brought them to the Americas in the 1550's and the English brought chickens to their American colonies in the 1600's.

Despite this long use of chickens, it was not until the nineteenth century that breeders began to improve the bird. Through developments in breeding and feeding, a meatier, more flavorful chicken can be produced in only 65 days. Chickens no longer need be Sunday treats—now they can be everyday fare.

**Nutritional value:** Chicken is an excellent source of good quality protein, yet is low in calories. Minerals, such as calcium, phosphorus, and iron, plus the B vitamins are found in this meat. Light meat has less fat, iron, and the B vitamins, riboflavin and thiamine, than the dark meat, but

more of the B vitamin, niacin. Young broiler-fryers will have even less fat than the older roasting and stewing chickens.

One serving of broiler-fryer before cooking averages 150 calories and of a roasting chicken averages 300 calories. Fat is found in layers just under the skin rather than distributed through the flesh. Calories can be minimized by removing the skin and using a recipe that does not add extra fat.

**Kinds of chickens:** Basically, chickens are divided into five categories according to age and weight. These categories are:

*Broiler-fryer or fryer*—Young tender birds weighing 1½ to 3½ pounds. Broiler-fryers may be roasted, simmered, baked, fried, grilled, or broiled.

*Capon*—Castrated roosters weighing 4 to 7 pounds and having large amounts of tender, flavorful white meat. They are roasted.

*Roaster*—Tender birds that weigh 3 to 5 pounds. They are roasted.

*Stewing chicken*—Mature, less tender birds weighing 2½ to 5 pounds and having more fat. Cook in liquid.

*Cornish game hen*—The smallest and youngest type of chicken, weighing 1½ pounds or less. Roast, broil, or fry these. Stuff before roasting, if desired.

Chickens are readily available fresh, frozen, and canned. Practically all that are sold in supermarkets are ready to cook. This means they are cleaned, eviscerated, and free from pinfeathers.

Fresh and frozen chickens are packaged as whole birds or as several pieces of one part, such as breasts or wings. Frozen products also include precooked chicken, either in pieces, as entrées with a complete dinner, or as the entrée alone; for instance, chicken with dumplings.

## Childhood favorite turns appetizer

← Dunking Dipper's Drumsticks, either hot or cold, into Zippy Pineapple, Royal Red, and Creamy Dill Sauces will be a hit at parties.

Canned products cover a wide range of items. Whole or boned pieces of chicken are available in cans. Foods made with chicken, including entrées, gravy, baby food, soup, and sandwich spread, are canned to serve many purposes. And new products are constantly being developed.

***How to select:*** Evaluate the cost in time and money when deciding which type of chicken to buy. Canned and frozen prepared dishes cost more than those made at home, but may be worth the expense if you have little time for cooking or want to be prepared for emergency meals. Packages of pieces are more expensive than whole chickens; again, the cost may be justified because like pieces cook in the same amount of time, or because your family prefers wings, legs, or breasts.

When buying fresh chicken, choose those with white or yellow skin that is thin, moist, and tender. Feel the flesh to see that it's plump and firm. Examine the breastbone to see if it is soft and flexible. Avoid chickens with off-odors for they are probably not fresh.

Grade and inspection marks are found on the label, wrapper, wing tag, or package insert and indicate the quality of the chicken. The United States Department of Agriculture grades A, B, and C appear in a shield-shaped mark. These grades indicate quality; Grade A is the finest and the most widely sold. A circular mark reading "Inspected for Wholesomeness by USDA" assures the consumer of a healthy bird processed under sanitary conditions. Federal inspection is required on all poultry transported across state lines.

Roast Chicken Elegante turns an ordinary meal into a banquet. Gingery orange sauce glazes the outside while a superbly seasoned stuffing of wild and long-grain rice bakes inside the bird.

### How much chicken to buy for a serving

Broiler-fryer.............¼ to ½ bird
Capon, roaster, stewing.....½ pound
Cornish game hen.........1 bird
Breast halves.............⅓ pound
Whole legs...............⅓ to ½ pound
Drumsticks or thighs........⅓ to ½ pound
Wings...................¾ pound
Backs...................⅔ pound

**How to store:** Refrigerate fresh chicken as soon as possible. Remove package of giblets from cavity of whole birds, cover the bird loosely in waxed paper or clear plastic wrap, and place in the coldest section of the refrigerator for one or two days. If not used within this time, freeze in moisture-vaporproof wrapping either whole or cut into parts. Frozen uncooked chicken will keep in the freezer 12 months.

Leftover cooked chicken should be chilled immediately and used in one or two days. It can be frozen for two to four months. Fried chicken, however, does not freeze satisfactorily. Never chill or freeze chicken with stuffing in it.

**How to prepare:** Chicken requires some basic preparation before cooking. Cut into desired pieces and rinse in cold water. Drain and if it is to be cooked in fat, dry to prevent spattering.

Frozen chicken is usually thawed before cooking. However, it can be roasted, fried, braised, or stewed without thawing, but this requires extra cooking time.

The best way to thaw chicken is in its original wrap, on a tray or pan in the refrigerator. A whole, three-pound bird will take about 12 hours to thaw. If you're in a hurry, thaw chicken in cold water: leave the chicken wrapped and immerse in cold water. Change the water often. It will take ½ to 1 hour to thaw small birds. Another method is to let the wrapped chicken stand at room temperature but do not try this in warm weather—it might spoil. Allow two or three hours per pound.

**How to use:** Chicken's wide acceptance makes it an excellent choice to serve at any meal. It's a welcome favorite to all ages in the family at a hearty breakfast, at dinner, or during a raid on the refrigerator. When serving guests whose food preferences are not known to you, chicken is one of your safest choices for the entrée.

### Chicken roasting chart

| Chicken | Ready-To-Cook Weight | Oven Temp. | Roasting Time Stuffed and Unstuffed | Special Instructions |
|---|---|---|---|---|
| Broiler-fryer Roaster | 1½-2 pounds<br>2-2½ pounds<br>2½-3 pounds<br>3-4 pounds<br>4-5 pounds | 375°<br>375°<br>375°<br>375°<br>375° | ¾-1 hr.<br>1-1¼ hrs.<br>1¼-1½ hrs.<br>1½-2 hrs.<br>2-2½ hrs. | Stuff, if desired, and truss. Place bird breast up on rack in shallow roasting pan. Rub skin thoroughly with salad oil. Roast uncovered. Brush dry areas of skin occasionally with pan drippings. |
| Capon | 4-7 pounds | 375° | 2-3 hrs. | Same as above. |
| Cornish Game Hen | 1-1½ pounds | 375° | 1½ hrs. | Prepare as above. Roast, loosely covered, for ½ hour, then, roast uncovered till done, about 1 hour. If desired, occasionally baste with melted butter or glaze the last hour. |

# Whole chicken

Whole chickens are ideal for roasting. This method takes little preparation time and produces a juicy, tender bird. For holiday meals, chicken is a good substitute for the traditional turkey—especially if your guest list is not large, or if some would prefer an entrée other than turkey.

Stuffed whole chickens make a grand meal whether served during the holidays, when entertaining, or for a family meal. Remember: the bird is not stuffed until just before it is roasted, and any leftover stuffing is put into the refrigerator as soon as possible after the meal.

## Cornish Hens with Rice Stuffing

     2  1- to 1½-pound ready-to-cook
        Cornish game hens
    ⅔  cup uncooked packaged precooked
        rice
     2  tablespoons dried currants
     2  tablespoons claret
    ½  teaspoon sugar
    ¼  teaspoon salt
        Dash pepper
        Dash ground nutmeg
        Dash ground allspice
     2  tablespoons slivered almonds,
        toasted
        Salad oil
        Wine Glaze

Season game hens inside and out with salt and pepper. In saucepan combine rice and ½ cup water; mix to moisten. Bring quickly to a boil, fluffing rice with a fork once or twice. Add currants, wine, sugar, ¼ teaspoon salt, dash pepper, nutmeg, and allspice. Cover and return to boiling, remove from heat. Let stand 10 minutes. Add slivered almonds.

Lightly stuff birds with rice mixture. Place breast up on rack in shallow baking pan. Brush with salad oil. Roast, covered, at 375° for 30 minutes. Uncover and continue roasting till drumstick can be easily twisted in socket, about 1 hour; occasionally basting with wine glaze. Makes 2 servings.

*Wine Glaze:* Combine ¼ cup claret; 3 tablespoons butter or margarine, melted; and 1½ teaspoons lemon juice. Brush hens with glaze.

# Roast Chicken Elegante

*Festive for holiday or guest meal—*

     1  3-ounce can broiled sliced
        mushrooms
     1  6-ounce package long-grain and
        wild rice mix
     1  tablespoon instant minced onion
     1  14-ounce can chicken broth
     2  3-pound ready-to-cook whole
        broiler-fryer chickens
              • • •
    ½  cup light corn syrup
     2  tablespoons thinly slivered
        orange peel
    ¼  cup orange juice
    ¼  teaspoon ground ginger
              • • •
     1  orange, cut in thick slices
        Butter or margarine
        Cranberry-orange relish

Drain mushrooms, reserving liquid. In medium saucepan combine rice mix and onion; stir in chicken broth and the reserved mushroom liquid. Cook according to package directions. Stir in mushrooms. Lightly stuff chickens with rice mixture; skewer shut.

Tie drumsticks to tail. Place birds, breast side up, on rack in shallow baking pan; tuck wings under or tie across back. Roast stuffed chickens at 375° for 1½ hours.

Meanwhile, combine corn syrup, orange peel, orange juice, and ground ginger. Brush chickens with corn syrup glaze and roast 15 minutes longer. Remove cord and skewers from each chicken; let chickens stand on warm serving platter a few minutes before carving.

For garnish, cook thick orange slices in butter till warm; then top with cranberry-orange relish. Arrange slices and parsley, if desired, around chickens. Serves 8 to 10.

# Sections of chicken

Chicken cut into halves, quarters, or pieces can be prepared in countless ways. Halves and quarters are a convenient size to broil or barbecue. Cut into smaller pieces, chicken combines well with other ingredients or makes a handy size to fry, stew, or bake. These pieces are also ideal for serving.

They are easy to handle, even for children, and one or two meaty pieces are a good amount for most servings.

Gourmet dishes around the world are made using cut-up chicken. The *arroz con pollo* of Spain and Mexico, *Kiev* of Russia, *coq au vin* of France, and *cacciatore* of Italy are but a few examples.

## Basic Broiled Chicken

Select two ready-to-cook broiler-fryer chickens (not over 2½ pounds each); split each chicken in half lengthwise or quarter. Brush with salad oil or melted shortening. Season to taste with salt and pepper.

Place, skin side down, in broiled pan (no rack). Broil 5 to 7 inches from heat, about 20 minutes or till lightly browned. Brush occasionally with salad oil. Turn; broil 20 minutes longer. When drumstick moves easily, chicken is done. Makes 4 servings.

## Honey Barbecued Broilers

*Display gourmet skills at an outdoor barbecue or use same sauce when broiling chicken indoors—*

    ¾ cup butter or margarine
    ⅓ cup vinegar
    ¼ cup honey
    2 cloves garlic, minced
    2 teaspoons salt
    ½ teaspoon dry mustard
    ½ teaspoon dried marjoram leaves,
        crushed
        Dash freshly ground pepper
            •  •  •
    3 2-pound ready-to-cook broiler-
        fryer chickens, halved lengthwise

Combine butter or margarine, vinegar, honey, garlic, salt, mustard, marjoram, and pepper; mix well. Place chicken, skin side down, on grill. Tuck wings under. Broil over low coals for 20 minutes.* Turn halves over; generously brush broiled side of chicken with honey sauce. Broil 10 minutes, turn, and brush second side with sauce. Broil 5 minutes more. Remove from heat. Just before serving, brush again with honey sauce. Makes 6 servings.

*Or*, use method for Basic Broiled Chicken.

## Delicious Baked Chicken

    1 2½- to 3-pound ready-to-cook
        broiler-fryer chicken, cut up
    2 tablespoons shortening
            •  •  •
    ½ cup sliced onion
    1 clove garlic, minced
    1 16-ounce can tomatoes
            •  •  •
    ¼ cup grated Parmesan cheese
    3 tablespoons all-purpose flour
    ½ cup dairy sour cream

Salt and pepper chicken; brown in hot shortening. Place in 12x7½x2-inch baking dish. Cook onion and garlic in 1 tablespoon drippings till tender. Add tomatoes; bring to boiling. Pour over chicken; cover and bake at 350° for 1 hour. Remove chicken to platter; sprinkle with cheese. In saucepan blend flour into sour cream; stir in drippings. Cook and stir till mixture thickens. Serve over chicken. Serves 4.

## Oven Herb Chicken

Cut up one 2½- to 3-pound ready-to-cook broiler-fryer chicken. Combine 1 envelope onion salad dressing mix; ½ cup butter or margarine, softened; and 1 teaspoon paprika. With spatula spread mixture over chicken pieces, then roll in ¾ cup fine dry bread crumbs. Sprinkle with paprika. Bake, skin side up, in greased large shallow baking pan at 375° till done, about 1 hour. Do not turn pieces during baking. Makes 4 servings.

## Barbecued Chicken

In skillet brown slowly in ¼ cup salad oil, one 2½- to 3-pound ready-to-cook broiler-fryer chicken, cut up. Place in 12x7½x2-inch baking dish. To skillet add ½ cup chopped onion and ¼ cup chopped celery; cook till tender. Add ½ cup catsup, ⅓ cup water, 2 tablespoons lemon juice, 1 tablespoon *each* brown sugar, Worcestershire sauce, vinegar, and prepared mustard. Season with salt and pepper. Simmer 15 minutes; skim off excess fat. Pour sauce over chicken. Bake, uncovered, at 325° till done, about 1¼ hours. Baste 3 or 4 times during baking. Makes 3 or 4 servings.

## Perfect Fried Chicken

⅓ cup all-purpose flour
1 teaspoon paprika
1 teaspoon salt
¼ teaspoon pepper
1 2½- to 3-pound ready-to-cook
   broiler-fryer chicken, cut up
   Shortening for frying

Combine flour, paprika, salt, and pepper in paper or plastic bag; add 2 or 3 pieces of chicken at a time and shake. Heat shortening (¼ inch deep in skillet) till a drop of water sizzles.

Brown meaty pieces first; then add remaining pieces (don't crowd). Brown one side; turn with tongs. When lightly browned, 15 to 20 minutes, reduce heat; cover tightly. (If cover isn't tight, add 1 tablespoon water.) Cook until tender, 30 to 40 minutes. Cook, uncovered, during the last 10 minutes. Makes 4 servings.

*Note:* Add ½ cup fine dry bread crumbs to flour for more crusty coating.

## Oven Fried Chicken

Cut up one 2½- to 3-pound ready-to-cook broiler-fryer chicken. Dip pieces in ½ cup melted butter or margarine; roll in mixture of 2 cups crushed potato chips (*or* 2 cups crushed barbecue chips, or crushed cornflakes, or 3 cups crisp rice cereal, crushed), ¼ teaspoon garlic salt, and dash pepper. Place pieces, skin side up, not touching, in greased large shallow baking pan. Sprinkle with remaining butter and crumbs. Bake at 375° till done, about 1 hour. Do not turn. Makes 4 servings.

## Dipper's Drumsticks

¾ cup all-purpose flour
1 tablespoon paprika
18 to 24 chicken drumsticks
     •   •   •
   Shortening for frying
   Zippy Pineapple Sauce
   Royal Red Sauce
   Creamy Dill Sauce

Combine flour, 1 tablespoon salt, paprika, and ¼ teaspoon pepper in plastic or paper bag; add 2 or 3 drumsticks at a time, and shake to coat.

Heat shortening (¼ inch deep in skillet) till a drop of water sizzles. Brown drumsticks on all sides, avoiding overcrowding—use 2 skillets, if necessary. Turn chicken with tongs. When lightly browned, 15 to 20 minutes, reduce heat; cover tightly. (If cover is not tight, add 1 tablespoon water.) Cook 30 minutes; uncover and cook 10 minutes longer. Serve drumsticks hot or chilled with sauces.

*Zippy Pineapple Sauce:* In saucepan combine one 12-ounce jar (1 cup) pineapple preserves, ¼ cup prepared mustard, and ¼ cup prepared horseradish; blend together. Heat the sauce through. Makes 1½ cups sauce.

*Royal Red Sauce:* In saucepan combine ½ cup extra-hot catsup and 6 tablespoons butter or margarine; heat just till blended. Makes about ¾ cup Royal Red Sauce.

*Creamy Dill Sauce:* Combine ½ cup dairy sour cream, ¼ cup mayonnaise or salad dressing, and ¼ teaspoon dried dillweed, crushed. Let sauce stand at room temperature for 1 hour before serving to blend flavors. Makes ¾ cup.

## Chicken Parisienne

6 medium chicken breasts
½ cup dry white wine
1 10½-ounce can condensed
   cream of mushroom soup
1 3-ounce can sliced mushrooms,
   drained
   Paprika
1 cup dairy sour cream
   Hot cooked rice

Place chicken breasts, skin side up, in 12x7½x2-inch baking dish; sprinkle with salt. Blend wine into mushroom soup; add mushrooms and pour over chicken. Bake at 350° for 1 to 1¼ hours. Remove chicken to heated platter; sprinkle with paprika. Pour sauce into saucepan; blend in sour cream and heat gently till hot. Serve mushroom sauce over chicken and hot cooked rice. Makes 6 servings.

## *Grilled to perfection*

Brush chicken halves with honey sauce that →
has a hint of herbs to accentuate the delicate flavor of Honey Barbecued Broilers.

## Rolled Chicken Washington

- ½ cup finely chopped fresh mushrooms
- 2 tablespoons butter or margarine
- 2 tablespoons all-purpose flour
- ½ cup light cream
  Dash cayenne
- 5 ounces sharp natural Cheddar cheese, shredded (1¼ cups)
- 6 boned whole chicken breasts
  All-purpose flour
- 2 slightly beaten eggs
- ¾ cup fine dry bread crumbs

Cook mushrooms in butter 5 minutes. Blend in the 2 tablespoons flour; stir in cream. Add ¼ teaspoon salt and cayenne; cook and stir till mixture is very thick. Stir in cheese; cook over very low heat, stirring till cheese melts. Turn into pie plate. Cover; chill 1 hour. Cut into 6 pieces; shape into short sticks.

Remove skin from chicken breasts. Place each piece, boned side up, between clean plastic wrap. (Overlap meat where split.) Pound out from the center with wood mallet to form cutlets not quite ¼ inch thick. Peel off wrap. Sprinkle meat with salt. Place a cheese stick on each piece. Tucking in the sides, roll as for jelly roll. Press to seal well. Dust rolls with flour; dip in egg, then in crumbs. Cover and chill thoroughly—at least 1 hour.

An hour before serving, fry rolls in deep, hot fat (375°) for 5 minutes; drain on paper toweling. Bake in shallow baking dish at 325° for 30 to 45 minutes. Serves 6.

## Rolled Chicken Breasts

- 3 large chicken breasts, boned, skinned, and halved lengthwise
- 6 thin slices boiled ham
- 6 ounces natural Swiss cheese, cut in 6 sticks
- ¼ cup all-purpose flour
- 2 tablespoons butter or margarine
- 1 teaspoon chicken flavored gravy base
- 1 3-ounce can sliced mushrooms, drained
- ⅓ cup sauterne
- 2 tablespoons all-purpose flour
  Toasted sliced almonds

Place chicken pieces, boned side up, on cutting board. Working from center out, pound chicken lightly with wooden mallet to make cutlets about ¼ inch thick. Sprinkle with salt. Place a ham slice and a cheese stick on each cutlet. Tuck in sides of each and roll up as for jelly roll, pressing to seal well. Skewer or tie securely. Coat rolls with the ¼ cup flour; brown in the butter. Remove chicken rolls to a 11x7x1½-inch baking pan.

In small skillet combine ½ cup water, the gravy base, mushrooms, and wine. Heat, stirring in any crusty bits from skillet. Pour mixture over chicken in baking pan. Cover and bake at 350° till tender, about 1 to 1¼ hours. Transfer chicken to serving platter. Blend the 2 tablespoons flour with ½ cup cold water. Add to gravy in baking pan. Cook and stir till thickened. Pour a little gravy over chicken; garnish with toasted sliced almonds. Pass remaining gravy. Makes 6 servings.

## Chicken with Dumplings

Prepare Stewed Chicken (*see page 494*). When chicken is almost tender, sift together 1 cup sifted all-purpose flour, 2 teaspoons baking powder, and ½ teaspoon salt. Combine ½ cup milk and 2 tablespoons salad oil; add to dry ingredients. Stir just to moisten. Drop from tablespoon directly onto chicken in boiling stock. (Do not let batter drop in liquid.)

Cover tightly; return to boiling. Reduce heat (don't lift cover); simmer till done, about 12 to 15 minutes. Remove dumplings and chicken to hot platter. Keep hot while preparing Chicken Gravy. Makes 10 dumplings.

*Chicken Gravy:* Strain broth from chicken. Measure 1 quart into medium saucepan. Heat to boiling. Combine ½ cup all-purpose flour and 1 cup cold water; gradually add to broth, mixing well. Cook, stirring constantly, till mixture is thickened and bubbly. Season with 1½ teaspoons salt and ⅛ teaspoon pepper. Pour over chicken and dumplings. Makes 6 to 8 servings.

### *Surprise waits inside crisp chicken*

Cutting into Rolled Chicken Washington re- →
veals the hot cheese. Garnish this entrée with grapes and parsley. Serve with baked rice.

# Ground or cubed chicken

Tasty sandwich spreads, salads, casseroles, appetizers, and soups are made with ground or cubed chicken. The meat can be purchased in cans or prepared by cubing a stewed chicken. Converting leftover chicken into a new dish by grinding or cubing will enable you to vary your menus and keep them interesting and creative. If preferred, freeze the ground or cubed leftovers for later use. (See also *Poultry*.)

## Stewed Chicken

*Excellent to use in salads or casseroles—*

> 1 5- to 6-pound ready-to-cook stewing chicken, cut up, *or* 2 large broiler-fryer chickens, cut up
> 2 sprigs parsley
> 4 celery branches with leaves, cut up
> 1 carrot, peeled and sliced
> 1 small onion, cut up
> 2 teaspoons salt
> ¼ teaspoon pepper

Place chicken pieces in Dutch oven or large kettle with enough water to cover (about 2 quarts). Add remaining ingredients. Cover; bring to boiling and cook over low heat about 2½ hours, or till tender. Leave chicken on bones in liquid for Chicken with Dumplings. Or, remove meat from bones. This will yield about 5 cups diced chicken for salads or casseroles.

## Chinese Chicken

> 1 medium green pepper, cut in strips
> 1 cup bias cut celery
> 2 tablespoons butter or margarine
> 1 10½-ounce can condensed cream of chicken soup
> ⅓ cup water
> 2 tablespoons soy sauce
> 2 cups cubed cooked chicken
> 1 16-ounce can chop suey vegetables, drained
> Hot cooked rice

In a saucepan cook green pepper and celery in butter till crisp-tender. Stir in cream of chicken soup, water, and soy sauce. Add chicken and chop suey vegetables; heat through. Serve over hot cooked rice. Pass additional soy sauce, if desired. Makes 6 servings.

## Club Chicken Casserole

In saucepan melt ¼ cup butter or margarine; blend in ¼ cup all-purpose flour. Add one 14½-ounce can evaporated milk (1⅔ cups), 1 cup chicken broth, and ½ cup water; cook quickly, stirring constantly, till thickened and bubbly.

Add to mixture 3 cups cooked long-grain rice; 2½ cups diced cooked chicken; one 3-ounce can sliced mushrooms, drained; ⅓ cup chopped green pepper; ¼ cup chopped canned pimiento; and 1½ teaspoons salt.

Pour mixture into a greased 2-quart casserole. Bake, uncovered, at 350° till heated through, about 40 minutes. If desired, top Club Chicken Casserole with ¼ cup toasted slivered almonds. Makes 8 to 10 servings.

## Chicken Chip Bake

> 2 cups cubed cooked chicken
> 2 cups sliced celery
> ¾ cup mayonnaise or salad dressing
> ⅓ cup toasted slivered almonds
> 2 teaspoons grated onion
> 2 tablespoons lemon juice
> ½ teaspoon salt
>
> • • •
>
> 2 ounces process American cheese, shredded (½ cup)
> 1 cup crushed potato chips

Combine all ingredients except shredded cheese and potato chips. Pile lightly in 1½-quart casserole. Sprinkle with cheese, then with potato chips. Bake at 425° till heated through, about 20 minutes. Makes 5 or 6 servings.

## *Quick family casserole*

Beginners will find Chicken Chip Bake easy → to make and will love the praise for this rich-flavored dish full of crunchy bits.

## Chicken Croquettes

    3 tablespoons butter or margarine
    ¼ cup all-purpose flour
    ½ cup milk
    ½ cup chicken broth
    1 tablespoon minced parsley
    1 teaspoon lemon juice
    1 teaspoon grated onion
      Dash paprika
      Dash ground nutmeg
    1½ cups finely diced cooked
         chicken
    ¾ cup fine dry bread crumbs
    1 beaten egg

Melt butter; blend in flour. Add milk and broth. Cook and stir till mixture bubbles; cook and stir 1 minute longer. Add parsley, lemon juice, onion, paprika, dash pepper, nutmeg, and ¼ teaspoon salt. Cool mixture. Add diced chicken and additional salt to taste; chill.

With wet hands shape chicken mixture into 8 balls, a scant ¼ cup each. Roll in crumbs. Shape balls into cones, handling lightly so crumbs remain on outside. Dip into mixture of egg and 2 tablespoons water; roll in crumbs again. Fry in deep hot fat (365°) till golden brown and hot through, about 2½ to 3 minutes. Drain on paper toweling. Makes 4 servings.

Top Chicken Croquettes with white sauce made using chicken broth for half the liquid. Add ½ cup drained, canned peas to sauce.

## Curried Chicken Balls

*Appetizers with an oriental accent—*

    1 5-ounce can chicken spread
    2 tablespoons chopped chutney
    1 teaspoon curry powder
      Dash salt
      Mayonnaise or salad dressing
    ⅓ cup coarsely chopped almonds,
         toasted

Blend chicken spread, chutney, curry powder, and salt; add enough mayonnaise to moisten (about 2 teaspoons). Form into ¾-inch balls; roll each in chopped almonds; chill. To serve, spear with hors d'oeuvre picks; stick picks into an apple or orange. Makes 20 appetizers.

## Chicken Pinwheels

    2 5-ounce cans chicken spread
    ¼ cup finely chopped canned
         pimiento
    ½ teaspoon prepared mustard
    ¼ teaspoon curry powder
    1 unsliced sandwich loaf bread
      Butter or margarine, softened

For filling combine chicken spread, pimiento, mustard, and curry powder. Trim crusts from bread. Cut bread in 9 lengthwise slices ¼ inch thick. Spread each long slice with softened butter or margarine and 2 tablespoons filling. Roll as for jelly roll, beginning at narrow end. Seal with softened butter. Wrap in foil and chill. For pinwheels, cut in ⅜-inch slices. Makes about 6½ dozen pinwheels.

To save time at the last minute, make sandwiches ahead and freeze for a few days. Cut while frozen; cover and thaw before serving.

## Basic Chicken Salad

Combine 3 cups cubed cooked chicken, 1 cup chopped celery, and ¼ cup chopped sweet pickle. Blend together ½ cup mayonnaise or salad dressing, 1 tablespoon lemon juice, ½ teaspoon seasoned salt, and dash pepper; toss lightly with chicken mixture. Chill. Serve in lettuce cups. Trim with pitted ripe olive slices *or* hard-cooked egg slices. Makes 4 servings.

## Chicken-Noodle Soup

In saucepan bring 3 cups chicken broth to a boil. (Use broth from Stewed Chicken, canned chicken broth, or chicken bouillon cubes dissolved in water.) Add 1 cup noodles and cook till noodles are tender. Makes 4 servings.

**CHICKEN-FLAVORED BASE**—A blend of chicken extract and flavoring used to make soup, gravy, and broth or to season meat and vegetable mixtures. The base is available as a liquid, as instant granules, as a paste, and in gravy mixes. (See also *Gravy*.)

**CHICKEN-FRIED**—A method of cooking in which the food is coated with seasoned flour or dipped in egg, then crumbs and pan-fried. This coating produces a brown crust over the food. Thin pieces of meat, such as round steak, are prepared in this manner. These must be pounded to tenderize if not tender. Creamy gravy is usually served with chicken-fried meat.

Chicken-Fried Steak combines a crisp crust with juicy, tender meat. Serve as a main dish with a favorite vegetable, boiled and sliced. Add a tangy, molded salad, hot bread, and dessert of parfaits with cookies.

## Chicken-Fried Steak

> 1½ **pounds beef top round steak,**
>   ½ **inch thick**
>   1 **beaten egg**
>   1 **tablespoon milk**
>   1 **cup fine cracker crumbs**
>   ¼ **cup salad oil**

Pound steak ¼ inch thick; cut into 6 serving pieces. Blend egg and milk. Dip meat in egg mixture, then in crumbs. Slowly brown meat in hot oil, turning once. Cover; cook over low heat till tender, about 45 to 60 minutes. Season with salt and pepper. Makes 6 servings.

**CHICKEN LIVER**—A small, delicately flavored liver used in the same way as other animal livers. They can be fried, broiled, used in casseroles and meat dishes, or added to giblet gravy and stuffing. Cook till just done, for overcooking toughens the meat and dries out the flavor.

Chicken livers contain B vitamins, iron, and large amounts of vitamin A. Yet, one medium liver has only 75 calories.

Entice guests or family with Chicken Livers Portugal. The combination of chicken livers topped with a wine-flavored sauce and wild rice adds a gourmet touch to the meal.

Packages of the livers can be purchased fresh or frozen. When preparing whole chickens, the livers may be set aside, if desired, and frozen until there are enough collected to use them as a main dish.

## Chicken Livers Portugal

    5 tablespoons butter or margarine
    1 clove garlic, minced
    2 tablespoons minced onion
    2 tablespoons all-purpose flour
    1 cup canned condensed beef broth
    1 pound chicken livers
    3 tablespoons Madeira or Marsala

Melt *3 tablespoons* butter in a heavy saucepan or skillet; add garlic and onion. Cook till onion is tender but not brown. Blend in *2 tablespoons* flour. Add beef broth; cook and stir till sauce is smooth and thickened. Combine the remaining flour, ½ teaspoon salt, and dash pepper; coat livers with flour mixture.

In medium skillet brown livers quickly in the remaining butter; gently stir livers and wine into the sauce. Heat through and serve livers over wild rice, if desired. Serves 4.

## Chicken Livers en Brochette

    ¾ pound fresh *or* frozen chicken
        livers, thawed (about 15)
    3 tablespoons butter or margarine,
        melted
    ⅔ cup fine dry bread crumbs
    2 teaspoons butter or margarine
    ½ teaspoon onion powder
        Dash cayenne
    2 tablespoons Dijon-style mustard
    1 tablespoon catsup
    2 teaspoons Worcestershire sauce

Dip chicken livers in the 3 tablespoons melted butter or margarine; coat with the bread crumbs. Thread on 3 skewers. Place on greased broiler rack; broil 6 inches from heat for about 3 minutes on each side or till livers are tender.

Meanwhile, in small saucepan melt 2 teaspoons butter; stir in onion powder, cayenne, mustard, catsup, and Worcestershire sauce. Heat just to boiling. Serve with livers. Makes 3 main dish servings.

## Chicken Livers and Rice

    1⅓ cups packaged precooked rice
    ½ pound chicken livers, cut up
        Butter or margarine
    1 10-ounce package frozen
        chopped spinach, thawed
    2 tablespoons butter or margarine
    2 tablespoons Burgundy
    4 ounces sharp natural Cheddar
        cheese, shredded (1 cup)

Cook rice according to package directions. Brown livers in a small amount of butter. Combine rice, livers, spinach, the 2 tablespoons butter, wine, ½ teaspoon salt, dash pepper, and cheese. Spoon into a 1½-quart casserole. Bake, covered, at 350° for 25 minutes. Garnish with additional shredded Cheddar cheese, if desired. Makes 5 or 6 servings.

**CHICK-PEA**—A pealike seed, also known as garbanzo. (See also *Garbanzo.*)

**CHICORY** (*chik' uh rē*)—A thick-rooted herb with bright blue flowers. The plant is cultivated for its roots and bitter leaves.

Chicory is known by several names. Its old name was succory. Witloof, endive, Belgian endive, French endive, and escarole are sometimes confused with chicory and mistakenly purchased as such. The characteristics which distinguish chicory

Skewer chicken livers and broil for a crunchy main dish or appetizer. Serve Chicken Livers en Brochette with the savory sauce.

from the flat or bushy endive and escarole are its thin, elongated stalk, tightly folded leaves, and color—which is usually bleached white during growth.

*Nutritional value:* Chicory contains some vitamin A and minerals. The calories are low—only four in ten small leaves.

*How to use:* Chicory leaves that are crisp, bright, and fresh are the best to use. Store in the crisper of the refrigerator without washing. Rinse as needed and use within two days. The leaves are excellent to use in salads, or to braise or cook as greens and serve as a vegetable dish.

The chicory root, dried, roasted, and ground, is used as a coffee substitute or additive to coffee. It adds aroma and body to the flavor. The French, Spanish, and Creoles are particularly fond of the chicory flavor in their coffee.

This herb heightens the flavor of many foods when added for seasoning. Use it in gravy, meat loaf, and dressing. (See *Herb, Vegetable* for additional information.)

**CHIFFONADE** (*shif' uh nād', -näd'*)—1. A garnish of finely cut herbs and vegetables used with soups and salads. 2. A salad dressing consisting of French dressing, chopped vegetables, and hard-cooked eggs.

## Chiffonade Dressing

    ½ cup salad oil
    2 tablespoons vinegar
    2 tablespoons lemon juice
    2 teaspoons sugar
    ½ teaspoon dry mustard
    ½ teaspoon paprika
      Dash cayenne
    1 hard-cooked egg, chopped
    ¼ cup chopped cooked beets
    2 tablespoons snipped parsley
    1 tablespoon chopped onion

Combine salad oil, vinegar, lemon juice, sugar, ½ teaspoon salt, dry mustard, paprika, and cayenne in screw-top jar. Cover and shake. Add egg, beets, parsley, and onion; shake well. Chill. Shake again just before serving over vegetable salads. Makes 1 cup dressing.

**CHIFFON CAKE**—A light, rich cake made with salad oil instead of solid shortening. This was one of the first new types of cakes to be developed for centuries. Developed in 1949, it combines the richness of shortened cakes with the lightness of foam cakes. They are classified as foam cakes because there is no creaming of shortening and sugar and because stiffly beaten egg whites help to leaven the cake.

*How to prepare:* The basic method of making chiffon cake is quick and easy. The dry ingredients are sifted into a mixing bowl and a well is made in the center. Salad oil, egg yolks, liquids, and flavorings are poured into the well. Then the mixture is beaten into a smooth batter.

Egg whites are beaten in a second large bowl. The volume of the chiffon cake depends on beating the whites correctly. Be sure all utensils are free of grease. This will keep the whites from developing the volume that they should. Avoid using a plastic bowl which may retain a greasy film. Have the egg whites at room temperature so that a greater volume will be developed as they are beaten. Beat till very stiff peaks form—when a spatula is pulled through, a clear path should remain.

Pour the egg yolk batter in a thin stream over the entire surface of the egg whites. Fold gently into the egg whites. Use a rubber spatula with down-up-over motion, turning the bowl after each stroke. Always fold gently; never stir the batter.

The cake is baked in an ungreased pan. Ten-inch tube pans are normally used but small cakes can be baked in loaf or round cake pans. The cake is done if it springs back when pressed lightly with the finger.

Chiffon cake is turned upside-down to cool. This is necessary to keep the cake from shrinking or falling. When cool, loosen the cake around the sides and center tube with a metal spatula or knife and remove it from the pan.

*How to frost:* Chiffon cake may be frosted or left unfrosted, depending on personal preference and how it will be served.

The frostings used with chiffon cakes are usually light and fluffy. Seven-minute frosting, icings, and glazes are good to use.

Blend the flavors of maple, brown sugar, and walnuts with
light-textured cake for an elegant dessert. Maple Chiffon Cake,
decorated with tiny mums and grapes, highlights a fall meal.

Follow these rules for a perfect chiffon cake: Sift dry ingredients into bowl and make
well in center. Add liquids
in order listed. Beat smooth.

Beat egg whites till very stiff
peaks form. Pour egg yolk
batter in a thin stream over
the whites, gently folding to
blend. Bake in *ungreased* pan.

Invert tube pan to cool as
soon as cake is baked. When
cool, loosen sides with a spatula and turn upside down; remove pan. Frost, if desired.

In both texture and flavor, these light frostings suit the delicate foam cakes. The sturdy texture of chiffon cake can also support a butter frosting, but it is not suggested for other types of foam cakes.

Frosted chiffon cake is a flavorful, yet light, dessert or refreshment.

This cake, also, is rich enough to be served without a frosting. It's especially good with milk for snacks, to pack in lunch boxes, or to serve as a dessert at lunch or after a light supper. (See also *Cake*.)

## Maple Chiffon Cake

  2¼ cups sifted cake flour
  ¾ cup granulated sugar
  3 teaspoons baking powder
  1 teaspoon salt
  ¾ cup brown sugar
. . .
  ½ cup salad oil
  5 egg yolks
  ¾ cup cold water
  2 teaspoons maple flavoring
  1 cup egg whites (about 8)
  ½ teaspoon cream of tartar
  1 cup finely chopped walnuts
. . .
  ½ cup butter or margarine
  4 cups sifted confectioners' sugar
  1 teaspoon vanilla *or* ½ to 1
    teaspoon maple flavoring
    Light cream (about ¼ cup)

Sift flour, granulated sugar, baking powder, and salt together into mixing bowl; stir in brown sugar. Make a well in center of dry ingredients. Add in order: salad oil, egg yolks, water, and flavoring. Beat till satin smooth.

Beat egg whites with cream of tartar till *very stiff peaks* form. Pour batter in thin stream over entire surface of egg whites; fold in gently. Fold in nuts. Bake in *ungreased* 10-inch tube pan at 350° for 1 hour. Invert pan; cool. Prepare frosting and frost cake.

*For frosting:* Melt butter or margarine in saucepan; keep over low heat till golden brown. Watch carefully to prevent scorching. Remove from heat. Place sifted confectioners' sugar in mixing bowl. Beat in melted butter. Add vanilla *or* maple flavoring. Blend in light cream till of spreading consistency.

## Chocolate Chiffon Cake

  4 1-ounce squares unsweetened
    chocolate, melted
  ¼ cup sugar
  2¼ cups sifted cake flour
  1½ cups sugar
  3 teaspoons baking powder
  ½ cup salad oil
  7 egg yolks
  1 teaspoon vanilla
  ½ teaspoon cream of tartar
  7 egg whites

Thoroughly blend melted chocolate, ½ cup boiling water, and ¼ cup sugar; cool. Sift together flour, 1½ cups sugar, baking powder, and 1 teaspoon salt into bowl. Make well in center of dry ingredients. Add in order: salad oil, egg yolks, ¾ cup cold water, and vanilla. Beat till satin smooth. Stir in chocolate mixture.

In large mixing bowl combine cream of tartar and egg whites; beat till *very stiff peaks* form. Pour chocolate batter in thin stream over entire surface of egg whites; fold in gently. Bake in *ungreased* 10-inch tube pan at 325° for 1 hour and 5 minutes. Invert pan; cool.

## Golden Chiffon Cake

  2¼ cups sifted cake flour
  1½ cups sugar
  3 teaspoons baking powder
  ½ cup salad oil
  5 egg yolks
  ¾ cup water
  1 teaspoon vanilla
  2 teaspoons grated lemon peel
  ½ teaspoon cream of tartar
  1 cup egg whites (about 8)

Sift together flour, sugar, baking powder, and 1 teaspoon salt into bowl. Make well in center. Add in order: salad oil, egg yolks, water, vanilla, and lemon peel. Beat till satin smooth.

Add cream of tartar to egg whites; beat till *very stiff peaks* form. Pour batter in thin stream over entire surface of egg whites; fold in gently. Bake in *ungreased* 10-inch tube pan at 325° for 1 hour and 10 minutes. Invert pan; cool. If desired, frost with seven-minute frosting tinted with a few drops yellow food coloring and sprinkle with tinted coconut.

Satisfy everyone's taste and fit any occasion with glamorous chiffon pies. This colorful array of pies includes Pumpkin Chiffon, Daiquiri Pie, Raspberry Chiffon, and Chocolate Chiffon.

**CHIFFON PIE**—A fluffy, delicate pie made of stiffly beaten egg whites or whipped cream, egg yolks, gelatin, and flavoring.

The name chiffon describes the very light texture which develops from folding in egg whites or whipped cream. The delicate filling is supported by the gelatin.

Many variations of chiffon pie are possible. The crusts may be either a baked pastry shell or a crumb crust. Filling flavors can range from chocolate, coffee, and rum to fruit. Fruit fillings use fresh or frozen fruits and juices. Garnishes can also be varied for interest and to fit the occasion. Whipped cream, chocolate curls, nut halves, twists of citrus fruits, or berries are attractive on chiffon pies.

The technique for making chiffon pies involves following a few simple rules. To make a smooth pie, it is important to have the gelatin at just the right consistency—partially set but still pourable. Partially set gelatin and flavorings are folded into stiffly beaten egg whites or whipped cream. To obtain a full, fluffy filling, this gelatin mixture is chilled until it mounds slightly, then piled into a baked and cooled pastry shell or crumb crust. The pie is chilled till firm—several hours or overnight—and garnished as desired just before serving.

Chiffon pies are best served well chilled. Because of their light texture, coolness, and richness, they are refreshing summer desserts, and they are especially good for ladies' luncheons or other social occasions. (See also *Pie*.)

## Pumpkin Chiffon Pie

   1 envelope unflavored gelatin
  3/4 cup sugar
  1/2 teaspoon ground cinnamon
  1/2 teaspoon ground allspice
  1/4 teaspoon ground ginger
  1/4 teaspoon ground nutmeg
  3/4 cup milk
  2 slightly beaten egg yolks
  1 cup canned pumpkin
  2 egg whites
  1/2 cup whipping cream
  1 9-inch graham-cracker crust
     (See *Crumb Crust*)

In saucepan combine gelatin, *1/2 cup* sugar, 1/2 teaspoon salt, cinnamon, allspice, ginger, and nutmeg. Stir in milk, egg yolks, and pumpkin. Cook and stir over medium heat till mixture boils and gelatin dissolves. Remove from heat and chill till partially set.

Beat egg whites till soft peaks form; gradually add remaining sugar and beat to stiff peaks. Whip cream; fold into pumpkin with egg whites. Pile into crust. Chill till firm. Trim with whipped cream and walnuts, if desired.

## Daiquiri Pie

1 1/3 cups sugar
  1 envelope unflavored gelatin
  1/3 cup lime juice
  3 well-beaten egg yolks
  1/2 teaspoon grated lime peel
  2 drops green food coloring
  1/4 cup light rum
  3 egg whites
  1 9-inch *baked* pastry shell*

In medium saucepan, combine *1 cup* sugar, gelatin, and 1/4 teaspoon salt. Add lime juice and 1/3 cup water. Stir in egg yolks; mix well. Cook and stir over medium heat till mixture boils and gelatin dissolves. Remove from heat; stir in lime peel and food coloring. Cool to room temperature; stir in rum. Chill till partially set.

Beat egg whites to soft peaks. Gradually add remaining sugar; beat to stiff peaks. Fold in gelatin mixture. Chill till mixture mounds. Pile into cooled shell. Chill till firm, 4 to 6 hours. Top Daiquiri Pie with whipped cream and candy lime slices, if desired.

## Raspberry Chiffon Pie

Thaw and drain one 10-ounce package frozen red raspberries, reserving syrup. Add water to syrup to make 2/3 cup. Dissolve one 3-ounce package raspberry-flavored gelatin in 3/4 cup boiling water; add 2 tablespoons lemon juice and raspberry syrup. Chill, stirring occasionally, till partially set. Whip 1/2 cup whipping cream. Beat gelatin mixture till soft peaks form; fold in raspberries and whipped cream.

Add dash salt to 2 egg whites; beat till soft peaks form. Add 1/4 cup sugar gradually; beat till stiff peaks form. Fold egg whites into raspberry mixture. Pile filling into one 9-inch *baked* pastry shell*, cooled. Chill till raspberry filling is firm. Garnish with additional whipped cream and raspberries, if desired.

## Chocolate Chiffon Pie

  1 envelope unflavored gelatin
  3 egg yolks
  1/3 cup sugar
  1/4 teaspoon salt
  1 teaspoon vanilla
  2 1-ounce squares unsweetened
     chocolate
  1/2 cup water
  3 egg whites
  1/2 cup sugar
  1 9-inch *baked* pastry shell*
     Whipping cream (optional)

Soften gelatin in 1/4 cup cold water. Beat egg yolks till thick and lemon-colored. Gradually beat in the 1/3 cup sugar; add salt and vanilla. Combine chocolate and 1/2 cup water; stir over low heat till blended. Add softened gelatin; stir to dissolve. Immediately beat chocolate mixture into egg yolks. Chill, stirring occasionally, till mixture is partially set.

Beat egg whites to soft peaks. Gradually add 1/2 cup sugar, beating to stiff peaks. Fold small amount of egg whites into chilled chocolate mixture. Then spoon about *half* the chocolate over remaining egg whites; fold in just till blended. Repeat with remaining chocolate. If necessary, chill till mixture mounds when spooned. Pile into cooled shell. Chill till firm. Whip cream and garnish with whipped cream and chocolate curls, if desired.

*(See *Pastry* for recipe.)

**CHILI, CHILE, CHILLI** *(chil'ē)*—A very hot pepper of the *Capsicum* genus. They are the strongest of the *Capsicums*—the smallest peppers are the hottest.

Chilies, fresh or canned, have many recipe uses where their fiery touch lends just the right accent. They can be chopped and used in casseroles or dips or left whole and stuffed with cheese, then coated with a batter for a Mexican dish. Whole peppers can be pickled and served on a relish tray. (See also *Pepper*.)

## Chilies Rellenos Con Queso

*A favorite Mexican main dish, made with canned or fresh green chilies—*

Cut 3 canned green peeled chilies in half crosswise *or* use 3 fresh long green hot peppers. (To prepare fresh peppers, place on baking sheet in 450° oven till skins form black blisters, about 15 minutes, giving a quarter turn once. Peppers will be cooked. Cool slightly. Peel and carefully remove the stems and seeds; cut in half.) Stuff chilies with 4 to 6 ounces sharp natural Cheddar cheese, shredded (1 to 1½ cups). Coat the peppers with all-purpose flour.

Beat 6 egg whites till stiff, but not dry, peaks form. Add 3 tablespoons all-purpose flour and ¼ teaspoon salt to 6 egg yolks. Beat till thick and lemon-colored. Fold the egg yolk mixture into the beaten egg whites.

For each Chili Relleno, spoon about ⅓ cup of egg batter into ½-inch hot fat (375°) in skillet. Spread batter into a circle. As batter begins to set, gently top each mound with a cheese-stuffed chili. Cover with another ⅓ cup batter. Continue cooking till underside is browned, 2 to 3 minutes. Turn carefully; brown second side. Drain thoroughly on absorbent paper. Serve at once. Makes 6 servings.

**CHILI CON CARNE**—A dish originating in Mexico made with cubed or ground beef, chilies or chili powder, and usually, beans. The literal translation of the Spanish words is chili with meat.

Homemade chili is a popular dish for a cold day. It can also be purchased in cans with or without beans. Accompany with crisp relishes and crackers.

For Chilies Rellenos Con Queso, a cheese-stuffed chili pepper is set on a mound of egg batter that has been cooked in hot fat till set. Another mound of batter is then spooned over the pepper. When the underside has browned, it's carefully turned over.

## Chili Con Carne

    1 pound ground beef
    1 cup chopped onion
    ¾ cup chopped green pepper
    1 16-ounce can tomatoes (2 cups),
        broken up
    1 16-ounce can dark red kidney
        beans (2 cups), drained
    1 8-ounce can tomato sauce
    1 teaspoon salt
    1 to 2 teaspoons chili powder
    1 bay leaf

In heavy skillet cook meat, onion, and green pepper till meat is browned and vegetables are tender. Stir in remaining ingredients. Cover; simmer 1 hour. Remove bay leaf. Serves 4.

## *Mexican favorites*

Serve south-of-the-border specialties for→ dinner such as Chilies Rellenos Con Queso, Cheese Enchiladas (See *Enchilada* for recipe), and Mexican-Style Steak surrounding a mound of rice (See *Steak* for recipe).

**CHILI POWDER**—A blended spice containing ground, dried red chili peppers, ground cumin seed, ground oregano, and garlic powder. Ground cloves, ground allspice, or powdered onion are often added. No two manufacturers' blends are exactly alike.

This seasoning is an American invention. The basic blend we know today was developed by settlers in the Southwest.

Chili powder is used extensively when preparing Mexican-type foods. A dash adds flavor to main-dish recipes as well as to salads and appetizers. (See also *Spice*.)

## Chili Cheese Log

> 1 3-ounce package cream cheese
> 8 ounces sharp process American
>    cheese, shredded (2 cups)
> 1 tablespoon lemon juice
> 1/4 teaspoon garlic powder
>    Dash red pepper
> 1/4 cup finely chopped pecans
> 1 teaspoon chili powder
> 1 teaspoon paprika

Let cheeses stand till softened; combine with lemon, garlic, and red pepper. Beat till light and fluffy. Stir in nuts. Shape in roll 1 1/2-inches across. Sprinkle with mixture of chili powder and paprika. Chill. Let stand at room temperature 10 minutes. Serve with crackers.

## Chili-Bean Salad

> 2 16-ounce cans green beans,
>    drained and chilled
> 3/4 cup diced celery
> 1/4 cup small white onion rings
> 2 tablespoons pickle relish
>    Chili Salad Dressing

Combine beans, celery, onion rings, relish, and 1/2 teaspoon salt. Add Chili Salad Dressing; toss. Cover; chill 1 hour.

*Chili Salad Dressing:* In mixing bowl combine 2 tablespoons salad oil, 1/2 small clove garlic, 1/4 teaspoon chili powder, 1/8 teaspoon salt, and dash pepper. Let stand 1 hour. Remove and discard garlic. Add 1 tablespoon vinegar and 1 1/2 teaspoons lemon juice; beat with rotary beater. Chill thoroughly. Serves 6 to 8.

**CHILI SAUCE**—A relish made of tomatoes, onions, celery, sweet red or mild green peppers, and spices. Despite its name, chili sauce is not fiery hot in flavor. It resembles catsup, but it is not strained. Chili sauce can be purchased bottled, or prepared and canned at home. (See also *Sauce*.)

## Chili Sauce

> 1 peck tomatoes (12 to 14 pounds)
> 1 pound celery (about 2 bunches),
>    chopped (about 4 cups)
> 1 quart small onions, ground
>    (about 2 1/2 cups)
> 3 green peppers, ground
>    (about 2 1/2 cups)
>    • • •
> 6 inches stick cinnamon
> 2 pounds brown sugar (4 1/2 cups)
> 1 quart cider vinegar
> 1 tablespoon dry mustard
> 1 1/2 teaspoons ground cloves

Scald tomatoes; peel, core, and slice in chunks into large kettle. Cook 15 minutes; drain off *half* (about 6 cups) the juice (use for drinking or cooking). Add celery, onion, and green pepper; simmer about 1 1/2 hours. Tie cinnamon in cloth; add with brown sugar, vinegar, mustard, cloves, and 1/4 cup salt to tomato mixture.

Continue cooking 1 1/2 hours. Remove cinnamon. Fill hot pint jars to within 1/2 inch of top; adjust lids. Process in boiling water bath 5 minutes (start timing when water returns to boil). Label jars. Makes 9 pints.

## Chili-Cheese Mold

> 1 envelope unflavored gelatin
>    (1 tablespoon)
> 1 cup chili sauce
> 1 cup cream-style cottage cheese
> 1/2 cup mayonnaise
> 1/2 cup whipping cream

Soften gelatin in 3/4 cup cold water; dissolve over low heat. Combine chili sauce, cottage cheese, mayonnaise, and 1/2 teaspoon salt; add gelatin. Whip cream; fold in. Turn into 1-quart mold. Chill till firm. Unmold on serving plate; pass an assortment of crackers.

**CHILL**—To cool food thoroughly, usually in the refrigerator at above-freezing temperature. Food may also be chilled with ice.

**CHINESE ARTICHOKE**—An herb with a tuber that is eaten as a vegetable. Sometimes this vegetable is referred to as the Japanese artichoke or knotroot.

The knotty, white tuber grows two to three inches long. Pick fresh, firm artichokes and avoid discolored or soft ones. The Chinese artichoke can be cleaned, then cooked or combined with a salad dressing to eat raw as a salad.

**CHINESE CABBAGE**—A vegetable belonging to the mustard family, often called celery cabbage. The thick, compact white stalks somewhat resemble celery and are topped with light green leaves. The flavor is cabbagelike, but more delicate, milder, and sweeter. Chinese cabbage adds a special flavor and crispness to salads and the quickly cooked Oriental dishes.

The Chinese cabbage called *bok choy* vaguely resembles celery. The stalks are white but not as compactly bunched, and the leaves are deep green and large. *Bok choy* is used in Oriental dishes.

This long slender head that looks like celery is called Chinese cabbage. It can be eaten raw or cooked as a vegetable.

### Chop Chop Salad

> 1 medium head Chinese cabbage, thinly sliced (about 6 cups)
> 1½ cups cold cooked rice
> 1 10-ounce package frozen peas, cooked, drained, and cooled
> 2 cups diced cooked pork
> 1 5-ounce can water chestnuts, drained and sliced
> ½ cup mayonnaise
> ½ cup dairy sour cream
> 1 teaspoon celery seed
> 1 teaspoon monosodium glutamate

Toss together first 5 ingredients. Combine remaining ingredients and ½ teaspoon salt. Toss with salad. Chill till served. Makes about 6 main dish servings.

**CHINESE COOKERY**—A type of cooking that is often characterized by meticulous preparation and quick cooking of simple, attractive, well-blended mixtures. Fast cooking helps retain much of the original taste, color, and texture of the foods, particularly vegetables. It also produces the crisp-tender contrast in textures so characteristic of Chinese dishes.

Chinese cookery combines the ideas of four regional areas, each contributing to the national cuisine. Many of the dishes are simple, and the seasonings are uncomplicated. Chief seasonings are soy sauce, garlic, ginger, and sugar. Popular ingredients include rice, pork, chicken, duck, chicken stock, bamboo shoots, water chestnuts, Chinese cabbage, Chinese pea pods, and bean sprouts. Cornstarch is used to thicken sauces of many Chinese dishes, giving them a translucent appearance.

A basic piece of cooking equipment in Chinese cookery is the wok, a pan with a round bottom and sloping sides.

Chinese cuisine has become popular in both home-cooked meals and in restaurants. (See *Oriental Cookery, Wok* for additional information.)

**CHINESE FIREPOT, MONGOLIAN FIREPOT**—1. An Oriental main dish where guests cook their own food in broth at the table. 2. The name of the utensil used for cooking this Chinese dish. The cooker consists of a pan with a chimney through the center. The chimney is filled with charcoal which is lighted, keeping the broth in the pan simmering throughout the meal.

The food to be cooked can be cut, sliced, and arranged ahead of serving; the sauces to be used can be mixed and waiting. When guests are ready to eat, heat the broth in the pot and arrange the sauces and raw foods around the firepot. Each guest then uses chopsticks, bamboo tongs, long-handled forks, or wire ladles to pick up the desired food and holds or drops it into the simmering broth. Because the pieces of food are small, cooking takes a very short time. The guest removes his food and dips it into one of the sauces provided. After cooking is completed, eggs can be poached in the flavored broth and served to the guests. Otherwise, the final step is to dash some dry sherry into the broth and ladle it into small cups.

For dessert, try fruit, tea, and fortune cookies. (See also *Oriental Cookery*.)

## Chinese Firepot

   ¾ pound large raw shrimp, peeled
     and cleaned (about 12 shrimp)
   2 uncooked chicken breasts,
     skinned, boned, and sliced
     very thin across grain
   ½ pound uncooked beef sirloin,
     sliced *very* thin across grain
   ½ head Chinese cabbage *or* 1 head-
     lettuce heart, coarsely cubed
   1 cup cubed eggplant *or* 1 5-ounce
     can water chestnuts, drained
     and sliced thin
   1½ cups halved fresh mushrooms
   4 cups small fresh spinach
     leaves, with stems removed
   6 13¾-ounce cans (10½ cups)
     *or* 2 46-ounce cans chicken
     broth (not condensed)*
   1 tablespoon grated gingerroot
     *or* 1 teaspoon ground ginger
    Chinese Mustard
    Ginger Soy
    Peanut Sauce
    Red Sauce
    Hot cooked rice

Shortly before cooking time, arrange raw meats and vegetables on large tray or platter and fill bowl with spinach. Provide chopsticks, bamboo tongs, long-handled forks, or wire ladles as cooking tools for guests.

In a firepot heat chicken broth and grated gingerroot or ground ginger to a gentle boil for cooking meat and vegetables. (An electric skillet, chafing dish, or fondue cooker* can be substituted for the firepot.)

Set out small bowls of the dunking sauces. Each guest picks up desired food with chopsticks or tongs and drops it into the bubbling broth. When tidbits are cooked, they lift them out and dip into sauce on plate. (Add more broth if needed.) Serve individual bowls of hot rice and Chinese tea. Makes 6 servings.

*For fondue cooker, use two 13¾-ounce cans chicken broth and 1 teaspoon grated gingerroot or ¼ teaspoon ground ginger.

*Chinese Mustard:* In mixing bowl stir ¼ cup boiling water into ¼ cup dry mustard. Add ½ teaspoon salt and 1 tablespoon salad oil. For a more yellow color, add a little turmeric to the mixture. Makes ⅓ cup sauce.

*Ginger Soy:* In a saucepan combine ½ cup soy sauce and 1½ teaspoons ground ginger. Bring to boiling. Serve hot or cold. Makes ½ cup.

*Peanut Sauce:* In a bowl thoroughly combine ¼ cup chunk-style peanut butter, 2 teaspoons soy sauce, 1½ teaspoons water, ¼ teaspoon sugar, 1 drop bottled hot pepper sauce, and ½ clove garlic, minced. Slowly stir in ¼ cup water, mixing till smooth. Makes about ½ cup.

*Red Sauce:* In mixing bowl mix together 3 tablespoons catsup, 3 tablespoons chili sauce, 1½ tablespoons prepared horseradish, 1 teaspoon lemon juice, and dash bottled hot pepper sauce. Makes about ½ cup sauce.

**CHINESE GOOSEBERRY**—Another name for the small, brown, kiwi fruit, imported from New Zealand. The fruit is oval and about the size of a lemon. It makes a delightful addition to salads. (See also *Kiwi*.)

## Oriental cuisine

Meat, shrimp, and vegetables will simmer → in bubbly ginger-spiked chicken broth when Chinese Firepot is in the menu plan.

**CHINESE NOODLES**—Includes several varieties, each made from a different grain—wheat, rice, corn, peas—and used in Chinese dishes. In the northern part of China, wheat is grown as the staple instead of rice; therefore, noodles have become the staple in that area.

To the Chinese, noodles mean longevity, and they are often served at birthday celebrations. Chinese noodles are usually very long, although they come in a variety of shapes and sizes.

There are a wide variety of Chinese noodles. Cellophane noodles, which are transparent, gelatinous, and flavorless, take on the flavor of other ingredients in the recipe. Dried noodles, which are packaged like spaghetti, are cooked before using as an ingredient. Often the Chinese quick-fry the cooked noodles until they are crisp and brown. Fresh Chinese noodles are also available in some specialty shops. This fresh product should be tightly wrapped and kept chilled in the refrigerator until it is used.

Rice sticks resemble cellophane noodles, but they have a different texture. The squares of pressed or rolled dough used as the wrappers for Chinese egg roll or *won ton* are sometimes considered noodles. (See also *Noodles*.)

**CHINESE ORANGE**—A name sometimes given to the kumquat. (See also *Kumquat*.)

**CHINESE PARSLEY**—Another name for the fresh, green leaves of coriander, an Old World herb. The Spanish call it *cilantro*. It looks like parsley and is used by the Chinese mainly as a garnish for main dishes or in soups. Store in a plastic bag or in the crisper of the refrigerator.

**CHINESE PEA PODS**—A variety of peas with a thin, tender pod and tiny, underdeveloped green peas. As the name implies, the whole pea pod is eaten. They are also referred to by other names, such as snow peas, French peas, or podded sugar peas.

Chinese pea pods can be purchased fresh in some Chinese markets or frozen in most supermarkets. Fresh pea pods are perishable and should be refrigerated, then used as quickly as possible.

This vegetable requires very little cooking and should be crunchy when eaten. Chinese pea pods add an Oriental flair to the meal and can be served as a vegetable, added to salads, or combined with chicken for an elegant main dish.

## Peas and Almonds

In skillet cook ¼ cup chopped green onion with tops in 1 tablespoon salad oil till tender but not brown. Add one 7-ounce package frozen Chinese pea pods, thawed, and one 3-ounce can sliced mushrooms, drained. Toss and cook the mixture over high heat 1 minute.

Dissolve 1 chicken bouillon cube in ¼ cup boiling water. Combine 1 teaspoon cornstarch and 1 teaspoon cold water. Stir bouillon and cornstarch mixture into peas. Cook, uncovered, over high heat till mixture thickens and bubbles. Toss, adding 2 tablespoons toasted slivered almonds. Makes 4 servings.

## Chicken Breasts a la Vegetables

    3 large chicken breasts, halved
    ⅓ cup all-purpose flour
    ¼ cup salad oil
    ¾ cup coarsely chopped onion
    ½ cup sliced celery
    1 clove garlic, minced
    1 10½-ounce can condensed cream
        of mushroom soup
    ¼ cup dry sherry
    1 6-ounce can sliced mushrooms,
        drained (about 1 cup)
    1 5-ounce can water chestnuts,
        drained and thinly sliced
    1 7-ounce package frozen Chinese
        pea pods, thawed

Coat chicken with flour; sprinkle with salt and pepper. Brown in hot salad oil in skillet. Remove chicken from skillet.

In same skillet cook onion, celery, and garlic till just tender. Blend in soup and wine. Add mushrooms and water chestnuts. Bring to boiling. Return chicken to skillet. Cover; simmer 20 minutes. Add pea pods; cover and simmer 10 minutes more. To serve, spoon some of the sauce over chicken. Pass remaining sauce. Makes 6 servings.

Snow Peas with Water Chestnuts is an example of the Oriental method of stir-frying. This procedure keeps the Chinese pea pods crisp and colorful. Water chestnuts add extra crunch.

## Snow Peas with Water Chestnuts

½ pound fresh Chinese pea pods
    (2 cups) *or* 1 7-ounce package
    frozen Chinese pea pods, thawed
1 tablespoon salad oil
1 teaspoon soy sauce
1 medium clove garlic, minced
1 5-ounce can bamboo shoots
    (⅔ cup), drained
1 5-ounce can water chestnuts
    (⅔ cup), drained and sliced
1 chicken bouillon cube
¼ cup boiling water
1 teaspoon cornstarch

If fresh peas are used, wash and remove tips and strings. In a preheated medium skillet or wok, combine salad oil, soy sauce, and minced garlic. Cook over low heat till garlic has browned. Add fresh or frozen Chinese pea pods, bamboo shoots, and sliced water chestnuts. Toss and cook over high heat for 1 minute.

Dissolve chicken bouillon cube in the boiling water; add to vegetable mixture in skillet. Cover skillet or wok and cook mixture over medium heat for 2 minutes.

Combine cornstarch and 1 teaspoon cold water. Stir into peas. Cook, uncovered, over high heat till sauce thickens and bubbles, about 1 minute. Makes 4 servings.

Chinese pea pods add a special crunch to main dishes, such as beef tenderloin-vegetable mixture—fit for company. They are often used in Oriental recipes using the stir-fry technique. (See also *Pea*.)

## Chinese Beef Skillet

    1 7-ounce package frozen Chinese
        pea pods
    2 tablespoons salad oil
    1 pound beef tenderloin tips,
        sliced paper-thin across
        grain
              . . .
    1 tablespoon salad oil
    ¼ cup chopped onion
    1 small clove garlic, minced
    4 cups thinly sliced raw
        cauliflowerets (1 medium head)
    1 10½-ounce can condensed beef
        broth
              . . .
    2 tablespoons cornstarch
    ¼ cup soy sauce
        Hot cooked rice

Pour boiling water over frozen pea pods and carefully break apart with fork; drain.

Heat 2 tablespoons salad oil in skillet. Add *half* the beef and cook quickly, turning it over and over just till browned, about 1 or 2 minutes. Remove meat at once. Repeat with remaining beef in hot skillet. Remove beef.

Add 1 tablespoon salad oil to skillet and cook onion and garlic just a few seconds. Add cauliflower. Pour broth over and cook till cauliflower is crisp-cooked, about 3 minutes, stirring gently.

Mix cornstarch, soy sauce, and ¾ cup cold water till smooth. Stir into mixture in skillet. Add beef and pea pods. Cook, stirring constantly, till sauce thickens. Serve over rice. Pass additional soy sauce. Makes 6 servings.

**CHIPOLATA** *(chip uh läd′ uh)*—A small, chive-flavored, spicy sausage.

**CHIPPED BEEF**—Lean beef that is pickled, then smoked and dried. It is usually prepared from the top round and sliced paper thin. Chipped beef is another name for dried beef. (See also *Dried Beef*.)

**CHIP**—The term used to describe irregular bits of food chopped from a larger piece or wafer-thin slices cut from some fruits or vegetables, such as potatoes, turnips, carrots, squash, or bananas. These thin slices are deep-fried until very crisp.

**CHITTERLINGS, CHITLINGS** *(chit′ uhr-lings, chit′ lins)*—The thoroughly cleaned, cooked intestines of a pig used in some regional dishes, especially in the South. Chitterlings are usually boiled and may be coated with cornmeal and fried after they are boiled. (See *Afro-American Cookery, Variety Meat* for additional information.)

**CHIVE**—A seasoning belonging to the onion family. It is a perennial plant grown as an herb and often used for ornamental purposes in the garden because of its tiny, colorful, lavender flowers.

This plant has been in existence for several thousand years and is native to some parts of North America, Europe, and Asia.

The part of the plant most often used in cooking is the slender, young, tender, dark green, tubular leaves. These leaves grow back when cut, just like grass; the purple flowers won't grow if the chives are constantly being cut. Sometimes the small, flat bulb part of the plant is used.

Chives are available in several different forms and can be enjoyed all year-round. Purchase a pot of fresh chives at the market, and you can enjoy the touch of color it adds to your kitchen. When buying a chive plant, look for fresh, bright green leaves, tender and crisp. Some hints to help chive plants grow: keep them in a sunny part of the kitchen; water frequently; snip often to within two or three inches of the base. A pair of scissors makes cutting up chives easy work.

If plant growing isn't a favorite hobby, frozen chives are available at most supermarkets. They are cleaned, chopped, and come packaged in plastic cartons. Store these chives in the freezer in the original carton. To use, loosen top layer with fork and remove the amount needed.

Chives also come freeze-dried. They are cleaned, chopped, and flash-frozen, then dehydrated and packaged. Look for this item on the herb and spice shelves in the

Add the springlike flavor of chives whenever a mild onion flavor is desired. They make a colorful trim for soups, too.

supermarket and store it on your own herb and spice shelf. Freeze-dried chives will be rehydrated by the liquid in any dish in which they are used.

Fresh, frozen, or dried chives can be used interchangeably in almost any recipe —in cooked foods, add the chives at the last minute, if possible, for best flavor.

Chives' mild onion flavor can be used effectively with cheese and egg dishes and similar light or delicate items. They add distinctive flavor to sauces, salads, salad dressings, soups, breads, and vegetables, and are delicious in dips. Chives are also one of the ingredients in the classic seasonings, *fines herbs*. (See also *Onion*.)

## Chive Mayonnaise

      1 cup mayonnaise
    ¼ cup snipped chives
      1 tablespoon lemon juice
      2 teaspoons tarragon vinegar

Mix all ingredients and dash salt together. Serve with cooked fish fillets or steaks.

## Chive Butter

Mix together ½ cup butter or margarine, softened; 1 tablespoon snipped chives; 1 tablespoon snipped parsley; ½ teaspoon dried tarragon leaves, crushed; and ½ teaspoon dried chervil leaves, crushed. Spread the chive butter on French bread slices. Wrap in foil and heat at 400° about 10 minutes. Or use on hot corn muffins, biscuits, or vegetables.

## Chive and Corn Spoonbread

      2 cups milk
    ¾ cup yellow cornmeal
      2 tablespoons butter or margarine
      1 teaspoon salt
      4 egg yolks
      1 8-ounce can whole kernel corn
          (1 cup), drained
      3 tablespoons snipped chives
      4 stiffly beaten egg whites
         Butter or margarine

In saucepan scald milk; stir in cornmeal. Cook and stir till thickened. Remove from heat; stir in 2 tablespoons butter and the salt. Set aside to cool slightly.

Beat egg yolks, one at a time, into slightly cooled cornmeal mixture. Fold in corn, chives, and beaten egg whites. Turn into greased 10x6x1½-inch baking dish. Bake at 350° till golden brown, about 35 to 40 minutes. Serve with butter. Makes 6 servings.

## Swiss Potato Salad

      4 cups cubed, peeled, cooked
          potatoes
      1 teaspoon salt
      4 slices Swiss cheese (4 ounces),
          cut in narrow strips
      1 cup dairy sour cream
      3 tablespoons milk
      2 tablespoons snipped chives
    ½ teaspoon dry mustard

Sprinkle potatoes with salt; combine with cheese strips. In small bowl blend together sour cream, milk, chives, and mustard; pour over potato mixture. Toss lightly. Serve at room temperature. Makes 4 or 5 servings.

# CHOCOLATE

*The many forms available prove its popularity as a food
and versatility as a cooking ingredient.*

Chocolate is a versatile food made from the bean of the cacao tree. It is the name of a beverage made with chocolate and water or milk, and the name given by many to candy having a chocolate coating.

The origin of the words chocolate and cacao is as interesting as their uses. Both words come from the Aztec language. Cacao is derived from *cacahuatl*, the name of the cacao bean, and chocolate stems from *chocólatl*, the name of a beverage. In 1720 a Swedish botanist gave the cacao tree its botanical name *Theobroma cacao*, which means cacao, food of the gods.

Cacao trees were originally grown in Central America and parts of South America. One legend attributes their discovery to a thirsty Aztec who started sucking the juicy pulp around the seed in the cacao pod. When his thirst was quenched, he threw some of the seeds into the fire. Soon the fire was giving off a spicy aroma. His curiosity aroused, he tasted the roasted bean and decided he liked it.

Some authorities believe the cacao beans were grown in the Western Hemisphere more than 3,000 years before the Spanish first arrived there and were used by the Indians as food and money.

Whatever the original use of the bean, when Cortez landed in Mexico around 1519, he was treated to the delicacy, *chocólatl*—the cold, bitter, syrupy beverage—by Montezuma, who was the emperor of the Aztecs at that time.

### For an everyday or special occasion

←Semisweet chocolate in cake and unsweetened chocolate in frosting make Velvety Fudge Cake a double chocolate dessert.

The Spanish observed how this *chocólatl* was prepared and noted that the bean first was roasted and ground; then peppers, spices, and herbs were added. Later, the Spanish planted cacao trees in their New World colonies. When they decided to improve upon the beverage, *chocólatl*, they added sugar, vanilla, and cinnamon, and served it as a hot drink.

For nearly a century, the Spanish kept the production of chocolate a secret. Finally, the monopoly was broken. Some say that Spanish monks shared the secret with other monks in Italy. Others say that the use of the chocolate beverage in royal courts began its distribution across the Continent. And still others say it was after the marriage of a Spanish princess to Louis XIV that the French started using it.

In the mid-1600's chocolate-serving clubs sprang up all over Europe. Chocolate became a fashionable drink, probably because it was so expensive and only the rich could afford it. The cost was high because the beans were imported and because processing was done entirely by hand. Nevertheless, chocolate was in demand.

During the eighteenth century, a method for mass-producing chocolate was developed, and the price of chocolate dropped. No longer was the drink strictly for the wealthy people.

Chocolate was brought to America by New England traders. The first chocolate factory was built in New England near Dorchester, Massachusetts, in 1765. In 1828, the cocoa press—used to extract the cocoa butter—was invented. It made possible the development of molded bars for eating. In 1876 a Swiss invented a way of making milk chocolate. Later, a smooth fondant chocolate was developed to replace the earlier coarse-grained chocolate.

*Unsweetened chocolate*, also called bitter, cooking, or baking chocolate, comes in two forms—solid and semiliquid. The latter form needs no melting. These products, along with all chocolate products, come from cacao beans, which are shown at lower left.

*Sweet chocolate* is not only perfect for desserts, but delicious to eat as is. It comes in bars that are divided in sections, making it easy to separate if the recipe calls for part of the bar. Sometimes it's referred to as sweet cooking chocolate.

*Semisweet chocolate* pieces are just right for nibbling or cooking. They also can be purchased flavored with mint. This type is a little less sweet than sweet chocolate and also comes in bars or squares. The squares are used for chocolate-dipped candies.

*Milk chocolate* is used most often for eating and can be purchased in bar form, with or without nuts; in pieces; as candies; or in chunks. This lighter-colored chocolate has a milder flavor and can be used for desserts or melted as an ice cream topper.

**How chocolate is produced:** Cacao trees grow in tropical climates, in those countries near the equator. Some of the top growers are in West Africa, Brazil, Ecuador, Venezuela, and the Dominican Republic. In most cocoa-growing areas, the main harvest lasts for several months. Differences in climate can cause wide variation in harvest times from year to year, even in the same locations.

Cacao beans are about the size of almonds, and about 25 to 40 beans or seeds are embedded in the moist pulp inside a pod. The cacao tree is an evergreen, and pink, yellow, or white flowers grow in clusters on the trunk and main branches. The average cacao tree produces 20 to 30 pods in a year, each pod producing 1½ to 2 ounces of dried beans.

When ripe, the pods are cut from the trees by hand. They are then cut open and the seeds are scooped out. The next step is a fermenting process, necessary for flavor development. During this time the white, moist pulp disappears. The seeds are then dried in the sun or by artificial means before proceeding with next step.

To make chocolate, these dried beans are cleaned, weighed, blended, and then roasted to bring out their characteristic aroma. Next the beans are broken into little pieces, called nibs, and are separated from their outer shells. These nibs are more than 50 percent cocoa butter—an unusual vegetable fat. (Cocoa butter is a good keeper as it resists rancidity and is very stable.) This cocoa butter is liquefied and released by grinding, thus forming a chocolate liquor. This chocolate liquor is the basic substance in all forms of chocolate. The processing then continues, forming one of the following types—unsweetened chocolate, cocoa, sweet chocolate, milk chocolate, and semisweet chocolate.

**Nutritional value:** Chocolate is a source of fat and calories. One 1-ounce square unsweetened chocolate equals 142 calories; one 1-ounce square sweet chocolate, 133 calories; 1 tablespoon cocoa powder, 21 calories; 1 cup chocolate milk, 208 calories; 2 tablespoons chocolate sauce, 87 calories; and one 2x3x2-inch piece unfrosted devil's food cake, 165 calories.

Chocolate is a good source of quick, extra energy due to its easy digestibility. It has been taken along on many expeditions —to the tops of mountains, to the poles of the earth, as well as on space projects. Chocolate is one of the foods that is also included in survival kits for soldiers.

# Types of chocolate

Chocolate is available in several different forms, all of which need to be stored in a cool, dry place at a temperature less than 75°. At higher temperatures, the cocoa butter in the chocolate begins to soften and rise to the surface. Upon cooling, the coating takes on a misty gray cast known as "bloom." This will not affect the flavor, nor does it mean the chocolate is undesirable. When the chocolate is melted, it will regain its original color.

For best results always use the kind of chocolate called for in a recipe. Ingredients are balanced, particularly in baked foods, to bring out the most desirable flavor.

**Unsweetened chocolate:** When the refined chocolate liquor is poured into molds and allowed to cool, small, hardened squares form. These one-ounce squares are individually paper-wrapped and, most often, are used melted in baking and cooking. This product is known as bitter, baking, or cooking chocolate. Larger, 10-pound blocks of the unsweetened chocolate are also formed for commercial use.

Another unsweetened baking product is made of cocoa and cocoa butter or vegetable fats in a semiliquid form, needing no melting before use. The one-ounce envelope or packet equals one ounce of melted unsweetened chocolate and is referred to as no-melt unsweetened chocolate. It is ready to use as purchased.

**Sweet chocolate:** To make this kind of chocolate, sugar and additional cocoa butter are added to unsweetened chocolate. These ingredients are then blended together to make a smooth paste. In some blends, vanilla, mint, or other flavorings are included. The sweet chocolate is molded, cooled, and hardened into sectioned bars for use in cooking or for eating.

*Semisweet chocolate:* The processing is the same as for sweet chocolate, except that less sugar is added. It is available packaged in bars, squares, or in pieces. These pieces are processed so that they will melt easily in cooking or hold their shape during baking at moderate oven temperatures. Semisweet chocolate is also used for eating; and, purchased in paper-wrapped squares, it is often used as a dipping chocolate or for making various kinds of candy.

*Milk chocolate:* This kind of chocolate is made with chocolate liquor, sugar, additional cocoa butter, and milk or cream. Vanilla is sometimes added for flavor. These ingredients are blended together, then molded into various forms. Milk chocolate is available in bar form, in pieces, like semisweet chocolate, and as candies or chunks. Sometimes nuts, raisins, coconut, or other ingredients are included.

*Cocoa:* Cocoa is another product made from the chocolate liquor. Part of the cocoa butter is removed and the remaining product is ground and sieved to a fine powder. It is available as regular and Dutch-process cocoa. Both are unsweetened products. Ready-to-use cocoa products are also available, and these contain sweetening and other flavorings. (See also *Cocoa*.)

# Uses of chocolate

The cooking uses for chocolate are inexhaustible since its flavor is such a universal favorite. Chocolate is most commonly used in beverages and desserts and candies of all types. Sometimes it remains in pieces in the finished product; at other times it melts during the cooking process. To use chocolate effectively in many recipes, however, it must first be melted.

Extra care should be used when melting chocolate for use in a recipe to preserve its flavor. Because chocolate burns or scorches very easily—and develops an unpleasant flavor—it is important to remember that low heat must be used for melting any type of chocolate. Also, if it is heated too quickly, the chocolate may not melt smoothly and may produce a grainy, undesirable product.

Heat chocolate over hot, but not boiling, water until partially melted. Remove from heat and stir until smooth. Or, in a saucepan, heat the chocolate over a very low direct heat, stirring constantly.

Avoid adding a very small amount of moisture—a little steam, a bit of flavoring, or a bit of moisture—to the chocolate. This can cause the chocolate to stiffen or "tighten." Should this happen, the chocolate is not ruined. Revive it by stirring in a little vegetable shortening—not butter or margarine, for they contain a small amount of moisture. While a very small amount of liquid adversely affects melted chocolate, it can nevertheless be melted in the larger amounts of liquid called for in recipe ingredients.

Occasionally an emergency substitution of ingredients has to be made. Cocoa with the addition of fat can be substituted for unsweetened chocolate. The substitution is 3 tablespoons unsweetened cocoa powder plus 1 tablespoon fat equals one 1-ounce square of unsweetened chocolate.

*As a beverage:* Hot beverages made with chocolate are sure to be popular with the young crowd as a snack after school.

With the addition of coffee, a chocolate drink is turned into a mocha beverage, an adult favorite.

## After Dinner Mocha

  1½ cups water
  ¼ cup instant coffee powder
   3 tablespoons sugar
   1 1-ounce square unsweetened
     chocolate
   3 cups milk
    Whipped cream
    Sugar

In saucepan combine water, coffee powder, 3 tablespoons sugar, chocolate, and dash salt. Stir over low heat till chocolate melts. Simmer 4 to 5 minutes, stirring constantly. Gradually add milk. Heat and stir till hot. Remove from heat and beat with rotary beater till frothy. Pour into cups. Spoon dollop of whipped cream on each. Pass extra sugar and whipped cream. Makes 3 or 4 servings.

## Mexican Chocolate

    4 cups milk
    5 1-ounce squares semisweet
       chocolate, broken up
    6 inches stick cinnamon
    1 teaspoon vanilla

In saucepan combine milk, chocolate, and cinnamon. Cook over medium heat, stirring constantly, till chocolate melts and mixture is heated. Remove from heat; add vanilla.

Remove cinnamon sticks. Beat mixture vigorously with *molinillo* or rotary beater. Serve in warmed mugs. Makes 4 servings.

Beating Mexican Chocolate with an authentic *molinillo*, Mexican handmill, gives this chocolate beverage a foamy crown.

## Hot Chocolate

    2 1-ounce squares unsweetened
       chocolate
    ¼ cup sugar
       Dash salt
    1 cup water
    4 cups milk

Combine chocolate, sugar, salt, and water in saucepan. Stir over low heat till chocolate melts. Gradually stir in milk; heat slowly just to boiling. Beat with rotary beater. Serve in heated cups. Makes 5 cups.

***As a dessert or candy:*** If the last part of the meal or the between-meal snack is flavored with chocolate—whether it be a frozen chocolate dessert, a dessert from the oven, a velvety cake, a cookie or candy, or a creamy pie—it is almost guaranteed to be a huge success.

The frozen dessert can be as exciting as a chocolate chip ice cream flavored with molasses or a dessert from the freezer made with chocolate candy bars. Or, the baked dessert may be a puffy chocolate soufflé served with a sauce or a variation of an old-fashioned bread pudding.

## Choco-Mo Ice Cream

*Molasses ice cream with chocolate chips—*

Combine 1 tablespoon cornstarch and ⅔ cup water in a saucepan. Stir in one 14½-ounce can evaporated milk (1⅔ cups). Cook and stir till mixture boils. Beat 3 egg yolks till light. Stir small amount of the hot mixture into egg yolks. Return to remaining hot mixture in saucepan. Cook and stir till mixture is almost boiling. Stir in ¼ cup light molasses and dash salt; chill the mixture in the refrigerator.

Beat 3 egg whites till soft peaks form. Gradually add ¼ cup sugar, beating till stiff peaks form. Fold into molasses mixture.

Turn into 11x7x1½-inch pan. Freeze till firm. Break in chunks and place in bowl; beat till smooth with electric mixer. Fold in ½ cup semisweet chocolate pieces that have been finely chopped. Return to cold pan. Freeze till firm. Makes 8 to 10 servings.

Several different chocolate products are used in these two delightful recipes, Coffee Toffee Squares and Brazilian Chocolate.

## Coffee Toffee Squares

    1 cup chocolate wafer crumbs
    2 tablespoons butter or
        margarine, melted

        • • •

    ½ cup butter or margarine
    ½ cup sugar
    4 egg yolks
    1 1-ounce square unsweetened
        chocolate, melted and cooled
    2 teaspoons instant coffee powder
    ½ teaspoon vanilla
    4 egg whites
    ¼ cup sugar
    3 ¾-ounce chocolate-covered
        toffee bars

For crust combine crumbs and 2 tablespoons melted butter or margarine. Press into bottom of 8x8x2-inch baking pan.

Cream together ½ cup butter and ½ cup sugar till light and fluffy. Thoroughly beat in egg yolks, chocolate, coffee powder, and vanilla.

Beat egg whites till soft peaks form. Gradually add ¼ cup sugar, beating till stiff peaks form. Fold egg white mixture into chocolate mixture. Spread over crust.

Coarsely crush toffee bars. Sprinkle over chocolate mixture. Freeze till firm, 3 to 4 hours. Makes 6 to 8 servings.

## Chocolate Marble Squares

    1 cup vanilla wafer crumbs
    2 tablespoons butter, melted
    ½ cup butter or margarine
    1 4½-ounce milk chocolate candy
        bar
    4 beaten egg yolks
    ¼ cup sifted confectioners' sugar
    ½ cup slivered almonds, toasted
    4 stiffly beaten egg whites
    1 pint vanilla ice cream, softened

Combine crumbs and 2 tablespoons melted butter; press into bottom of 9x9x2-inch baking pan.

In saucepan melt ½ cup butter and candy bar over low heat. Cook and stir till blended. Stir small amount of hot mixture into egg yolks; return to saucepan. Cook and stir over low heat till thickened. Remove from heat. Add confectioners' sugar. Beat till smooth. Stir in *half* the toasted, slivered almonds; cool.

Fold into egg whites. Spoon over crust alternately with ice cream. Gently cut through to marble. Freeze till firm, about 6 hours. Cut in squares; sprinkle with remaining nuts. If desired, top with dollops of whipped cream, then sprinkle with nuts. Makes 9 servings.

## Chocolate Soufflé

In saucepan blend ⅓ cup light cream and one 3-ounce package cream cheese over very low heat. Add ½ cup semisweet chocolate pieces. Cook and stir to melt chocolate; cool.

Beat 3 egg yolks with dash salt till thick and lemon-colored, about 5 minutes. Slowly blend into cooled chocolate.

Beat 3 egg whites to soft peaks. Gradually add ¼ cup sifted confectioners' sugar, beating to stiff peaks. Fold small amount of whites into chocolate mixture. Fold chocolate, half at a time, into the stiffly beaten egg whites. Pour mixture into an *ungreased* 1-quart soufflé dish.

Bake at 300° till a knife inserted halfway between center and edge comes out clean, about 50 minutes. Serve at once with Custard Sauce. Makes 5 or 6 servings.

*Custard Sauce:* Mix 4 beaten egg yolks, dash salt, and ¼ cup sugar in heavy saucepan. Gradually stir in 2 cups milk, scalded and slightly cooled. Cook and stir over low heat till mixture coats a metal spoon. Remove from heat. Cool pan at once in cold water. Stir a minute or two. Add 1 teaspoon vanilla. Chill.

## Chocolate Meringue Pudding

*A different version of bread pudding—*

    2 cups milk
 1½ 1-ounce squares unsweetened
        chocolate
    3 cups 1-inch day-old bread cubes
  ¼ cup brown sugar
    1 teaspoon vanilla
    2 beaten egg yolks
    2 egg whites
    3 tablespoons granulated sugar
  ½ teaspoon shredded orange peel

Combine milk and chocolate in saucepan. Cook and stir over low heat till chocolate melts. Place bread in bowl; pour chocolate mixture over. Add brown sugar, vanilla, egg yolks, and ¼ teaspoon salt. Mix lightly to blend.

Lightly grease six 5-ounce custard cups. Set in shallow baking pan and fill with pudding mixture. Pour hot water 1-inch deep around cups. Bake at 350° till knife inserted comes out clean, about 30 to 35 minutes.

Meanwhile, prepare meringue. In mixing bowl beat egg whites till soft peaks form. Gradually add granulated sugar, beating till stiff peaks form. Fold in shredded orange peel. Remove puddings from oven. Add a dollop of meringue. Bake till meringue is lightly browned, about 10 minutes. Makes 6 servings.

Chocolate also is a favorite for use in cakes and frostings. Who can resist a luscious, velvety wedge of cake topped with chocolate frosting? The chocolate cake will appear more red if baking soda is used as the leavening agent, although too much soda will give an undesirable flavor.

## Velvety Fudge Cake

*This one is made with semisweet chocolate—*

    1 6-ounce package semisweet
        chocolate pieces (1 cup)
  ¼ cup butter or margarine
  ¾ cup sugar
    1 teaspoon vanilla
    2 eggs
 1½ cups sifted all-purpose flour
  ¾ teaspoon baking soda
    1 cup sour milk *or* buttermilk
        Creamy Chocolate Frosting

In small saucepan melt chocolate over very low heat, stirring constantly; cool. Thoroughly cream together butter or margarine, sugar, and vanilla. Stir in melted chocolate. Add eggs, one at a time, beating well after each. Sift together flour, baking soda, and ½ teaspoon salt. Add dry ingredients to creamed mixture alternately with sour milk *or* buttermilk, beating the mixture well after each addition.

Pour into 2 greased and floured 8x1½-inch round cake pans. Bake at 350° till done, about 25 to 30 minutes. Frost.

*Creamy Chocolate Frosting:* In small saucepan melt two 1-ounce squares unsweetened chocolate over low heat; cool. Beat together one 3-ounce package softened cream cheese and 2 tablespoons milk. Add 2 cups sifted confectioners' sugar; mix well. Beat in the melted chocolate, another 2 tablespoons milk, and 1½ teaspoons vanilla. Add enough additional sifted confectioners' sugar (about 2½ to 2¾ cups) to make frosting of spreading consistency.

## Chocolate Layer Cake

In mixing bowl cream ⅔ cup butter or margarine. Gradually add 1¾ cups sugar, creaming till mixture is light. Add 1 teaspoon vanilla and 2 eggs, one at a time, beating well after each. Blend in 2½ 1-ounce squares unsweeteneed chocolate, melted and cooled.

Sift together 2½ cups sifted cake flour, 1¼ teaspoons baking soda, and ½ teaspoon salt. Add to creamed mixture alternately with 1¼ cups icy cold water, beating after each addition. Pour into 2 greased and floured 9x1½-inch round cake pans. Bake at 350° till done, about 30 to 35 minutes. Frost.

## Sweet Chocolate Cake

　1　4-ounce bar sweet cooking
　　　chocolate
　⅓　cup water
　½　cup butter or margarine
　1　cup sugar
　3　egg yolks
　1　teaspoon vanilla
　　　　• • •
　1¾　cups sifted cake flour
　1　teaspoon baking soda
　½　teaspoon salt
　⅔　cup buttermilk
　3　egg whites
　　　Coconut Frosting

Combine chocolate and water in saucepan. Stir over low heat till chocolate melts. Cool.

Cream butter or margarine; gradually add sugar, creaming till light. Add egg yolks, one at a time, beating well after each. Blend in vanilla and chocolate mixture.

Sift together flour, baking soda, and salt. Add to creamed mixture alternately with buttermilk, beating after each addition. Beat egg whites to stiff peaks. Fold into batter. Pour into 2 greased and lightly floured 8x1½-inch round cake pans. Bake at 350° for 30 to 35 minutes. Cool. Spread Coconut Frosting between layers and on top of the cake.

*Coconut Frosting:* Combine one 6-ounce can evaporated milk (⅔ cup), ⅔ cup sugar, ¼ cup butter or margarine, 1 slightly beaten egg, and dash salt. Cook and stir over medium heat till mixture thickens and bubbles, about 12 minutes. Cool slightly. Add 1 teaspoon vanilla, 1⅓ cups flaked coconut, and ½ cup chopped pecans; mix well. Cool.

## Choco–Blender Frosting

Put 1 cup sugar in blender container; cover and blend at high speed about 1 minute. Add three 1-ounce squares unsweetened chocolate, cut in small pieces; one 6-ounce can evaporated milk (⅔ cup); and dash salt. Blend at high speed of blender till frosting is thick enough for spreading consistency, about 3 minutes.

If necessary, use rubber spatula to scrape sides of blender container. Makes enough to frost the tops of two 8-inch layers. (If firmer frosting is desired, chill frosted cake.)

Fill the cookie jar or candy dish with freshly made chocolate treats and watch them disappear. Cookies and candies can serve as an energy booster between meals or for dessert to satisfy a sweet tooth. Bar cookies, in particular, make good take-along desserts for lunch boxes.

## Chocolate Chippers

　½　cup shortening
　½　cup granulated sugar
　¼　cup brown sugar
　1　egg
　1　teaspoon vanilla
　1　cup sifted all-purpose flour
　½　teaspoon baking soda
　¾　teaspoon salt
　1　6-ounce package semisweet
　　　chocolate pieces (1 cup)
　½　cup chopped walnuts

Cream shortening, sugars, egg, and vanilla till fluffy. Sift together flour, baking soda, and salt; stir into creamed mixture.

Stir in chocolate pieces and chopped walnuts. Drop from teaspoon 2 inches apart onto greased cookie sheet. Bake at 375° for 10 to 12 minutes. Remove from pan. Makes 3 dozen.

## Double Chocolate Bars

Cream ¼ cup butter or margarine, ¾ cup sugar, and 1 teaspoon vanilla till fluffy. Add ¼ cup light corn syrup and continue creaming. Beat in 2 eggs and two 1-ounce squares unsweetened chocolate, melted and cooled.

Sift together 1 cup sifted all-purpose flour, ½ teaspoon salt, and ½ teaspoon baking powder. Stir into batter. Fold in one-half 6-ounce package semisweet chocolate pieces (½ cup) and ½ cup chopped walnuts. Spread in greased 9x9x2-inch baking pan. Bake at 350° for 25 minutes. Cut in bars when cool.

### *The all-American favorite*

Mint-flavored semisweet chocolate can be →
substituted in Chocolate Chippers for a new and different flavor sensation.

## Chocolate Swirl Cookies

½ cup butter or margarine
1 cup sugar
2 eggs
2 1-ounce squares unsweetened
    chocolate, melted
1 teaspoon vanilla

· · ·

2 cups sifted all-purpose flour
1½ teaspoons baking powder
½ teaspoon salt
½ teaspoon baking soda
½ teaspoon ground cinnamon
¼ teaspoon ground ginger
¼ teaspoon ground allspice
    Sugar

Cream butter and 1 cup sugar till light and fluffy. Add eggs, chocolate, and vanilla; beat well. Sift together next 7 ingredients; stir into creamed mixture. Blend well. Chill.

To form swirls roll about 2 teaspoons cookie dough on lightly floured board with hands to form a rope about 9 inches long. Carefully place on cookie sheet and coil into spiral shape. Sprinkle with sugar. Bake at 350° for 10 minutes. Makes about 5 dozen.

## Chocolate Cherries

Drain one 8-ounce jar whole maraschino cherries thoroughly on paper toweling. Prepare one 12-ounce package chocolate fudge mix according to package directions, *except* leave mixture over simmering water after it becomes glossy. Using fork, dip each cherry into fudge mixture, turning to coat evenly. Push onto waxed paper with another fork. Stir fudge mixture frequently. Pour remaining fudge into a small buttered pan. Makes 2½ dozen.

*Note:* These will not freeze or store well.

Chocolate pies are always appreciated and enjoyed, whether they get a quick head start with convenience products, such as pudding or dessert mixes, or are made from scratch.

To trim the tops of pies or cakes with chocolate curls, use a 4-ounce bar of sweet cooking chocolate at room temperature. Using a vegetable peeler, carefully shave off thin slices of the chocolate and watch it curl as it is being cut. The temperature of the chocolate is very important—if too cold, the chocolate curls will break. If the chocolate is breaking into shreds as it is being cut, it may help to dip the vegetable peeler in warm water.

## Chocolate-Flecked Chiffon Pie

1 envelope unflavored gelatin
1 cup sugar
1 cup milk
2 1-ounce squares unsweetened
    chocolate
2 2-ounce packages dessert topping
    mix *or* 2 cups whipping cream
1 *baked* 9-inch pastry shell
    (See *Pastry*)

Combine gelatin, sugar, and dash salt in saucepan. Add milk; cut chocolate in small pieces and add. Cook and stir over medium heat till gelatin is dissolved and chocolate is melted. (Mixture will be chocolate flecked.) Chill, stirring occasionally, till mixture mounds.

Prepare dessert topping mix according to package directions or whip cream. Fold into gelatin mixture. Pile into cooled pastry shell. Chill till firm. If desired, trim with additional whipped cream and chocolate curls.

## Chocolate Peanut Pie

1 4-ounce package *regular* chocolate
    pudding mix
¼ cup peanut butter
1 2-ounce package dessert
    topping mix
1 *baked* 9-inch pastry shell
    (See *Pastry*)
2 tablespoons peanuts, chopped

Prepare pudding mix according to package directions, *except use only 1¾ cups milk.* Add small amount of hot pudding to peanut butter; beat till smooth. Beat into remaining pudding. Cover surface and cool, stirring once or twice. Prepare topping mix according to package directions; reserve ½ cup. Fold remaining topping into pudding. Pile into pastry shell; chill. Top with reserved dessert topping and nuts.

## Chocolate Cheese Pie

1½ cups fine graham cracker crumbs
½ cup melted butter or margarine

• • •

1 6-ounce package semisweet
   chocolate pieces (1 cup)
2 3-ounce packages cream cheese,
   softened
½ cup sugar
1 teaspoon vanilla
¼ teaspoon salt
2 egg yolks
1 cup whipping cream
2 egg whites
¼ cup sugar

Mix cracker crumbs and melted butter or margarine; press into a 9-inch pie plate. Chill.

Melt chocolate pieces over hot, *not boiling*, water. Cool slightly. Blend cream cheese, ½ cup sugar, vanilla, and salt. Add egg yolks, one at a time, beating well after each. Stir in melted chocolate; chill till thick. Beat smooth.

Whip cream; fold cream into chocolate. Beat egg whites to soft peaks. Gradually add ¼ cup sugar, beating till stiff peaks form; fold into chocolate. Pile into crust. Place in freezer till well chilled; remove 5 to 10 minutes before serving. Makes 8 servings.

# Chocolate products

In addition to the basic types of chocolate, there are commercial products that use chocolate for flavoring or as the main ingredient in the product.

*Chocolate chip:* One of the names given to a semisweet chocolate piece that is small, and uniformly sized and shaped.

*Chocolate dairy drink:* A dairy-produced beverage made of skimmed milk or partially skimmed milk, flavored with chocolate syrup or cocoa and sweetened. An 8-ounce glass contains about 190 calories.

*Chocolate decorative candy:* The name given to uniformly shaped ⅛- to ¼-inch long slender pieces of semisweet chocolate used for decorating cakes, cookies, or other desserts. They retain their shape during oven baking at moderate temperatures.

Create a luscious sundae with chocolate and vanilla ice cream. Then spoon Easy Chocolate Sauce and walnuts over the top.

*Chocolate milk:* A beverage made of whole milk flavored with chocolate syrup or powder and sweetened. An 8-ounce glass of chocolate milk contains about 213 calories. Cold chocolate milk is a delightful drink as is, or it can be heated and used as the base for other beverages.

## Spiced Chocolate Coffee

*A simple and jiffy recipe to prepare—*

2 tablespoons instant coffee
   powder
   Dash ground cinnamon
1 cup water
2 cups chocolate milk
   Sweetened whipped cream

Combine coffee powder and cinnamon in small saucepan. Stir in water and chocolate milk. Heat, stirring constantly, till piping hot. Pour into small cups and put a spoonful of sweetened whipped cream atop each serving. Makes six ½-cup servings.

*Chocolate sauce:* A dessert sauce that can be prepared at home or purchased at the store. Chocolate or cocoa and sugar are the basic ingredients, with milk or cream as the liquid, and corn syrup or butter as possible additions. Other flavorings are occasionally added. You might enjoy flavor blends such as chocolate-mint, chocolate-caramel, or others found in the store.

## Easy Chocolate Sauce

In small heavy saucepan heat one 6-ounce package semisweet chocolate pieces (1 cup) and ½ cup evaporated milk over medium heat, stirring constantly till blended. Serve warm or at room temperature. Makes 1 cup.

## Regal Chocolate Sauce

    ½ cup light corn syrup
    1 cup sugar
    3 1-ounce squares unsweetened
        chocolate, broken up
    1 teaspoon vanilla
    ½ cup evaporated milk

Chocolate syrup (right) and sauce (left) are closely related except chocolate sauce has milk, cream, and/or butter added.

Combine corn syrup, sugar, and 1 cup water in saucepan. Cook to soft-ball stage (236°). Remove from heat. Add chocolate; stir till melted. Add vanilla. Slowly add evaporated milk; mix thoroughly. Cool. Makes 1¾ cups.

*Chocolate syrup:* A thin chocolate- or cocoa-flavored syrup made with sugar, water, salt, and other flavorings. The syrup is often used as the flavor base for making beverages, frozen desserts, or ice cream sodas, and can be used as an ice cream topper. Chocolate syrup is available in jars and cans at supermarkets, or it can be prepared at home.

## Chocolate Syrup

    ½ cup sugar
    ¼ cup unsweetened cocoa powder
        Dash salt
    ½ cup water
    1 teaspoon vanilla

Mix sugar, cocoa powder, and salt in saucepan. Add water. Bring to boiling. Reduce heat and cook 1 minute. Remove from heat and add vanilla. Cool. Store in refrigerator. Makes ⅔ cup. (For a quick beverage, combine 2 tablespoons syrup and 1 cup milk. Heat. Serves 1.)

## Brazilian Chocolate

*A good breakfast beverage—*

    ½ cup chocolate syrup
    ¼ teaspoon salt
    ¼ teaspoon ground cinnamon
    2 tablespoons instant coffee
        powder
    2 cups hot water
    2 cups hot milk
    1 teaspoon vanilla

In saucepan combine syrup, salt, cinnamon, and coffee powder. Stir in ¼ *cup* of the water; cook over medium-low heat till heated through. Add remaining water and milk. Cook just till heated through, stirring occasionally. Add vanilla; beat with rotary beater till foamy. Serve immediately. Makes 6 servings.

A cross-bladed, rocker-type chopper and a small wooden bowl make chopping a small quantity of nuts quick and easy.

Chop with a French chef's knife. Place fingertips on top of blade near point. Rock knife up and down, pivoting on point.

**CHOKECHERRY**—The fruit of a wild cherry tree native to North America. The fruit is sharp in flavor and is best used in jelly or jam to be served on slices of toast.

**CHOLESTEROL**—A fatlike substance present in all animal cells and an essential component of the blood and other parts of the body. Manufactured by the liver and other organs, cholesterol regulates the passage of substances through the cell walls of the body.

Cholesterol is present in meat fat, egg yolks, liver, brains, kidneys, shellfish, and dairy fats. The body's cholesterol level and types of fat consumed are being studied in the search for causes of hardening of the arteries and heart disease. Results of these investigations, however, are incomplete.

**CHOP**—1. The motion of cutting food with a knife, chopper, or blender into small pieces about the size of peas. 2. Individual cuts of meat from the loin or rib areas, consisting of bone and tender muscle. It usually refers to lamb, veal, or pork.

**CHOP SUEY**—A main dish with an Oriental name and ingredients, but of American origin. It may include pieces of pork or poultry, bean sprouts, bamboo shoots, water chestnuts, soy sauce, and mushrooms, and is served with rice. Chop suey is also available as a canned or frozen product. (See also *Oriental Cookery*.)

### Turkey Chop Suey

½ cup sliced onion
2 tablespoons butter or margarine
2 cups diced cooked turkey
2 cups chicken broth
1 cup sliced celery
1 5-ounce can water chestnuts, drained and thinly sliced
3 tablespoons soy sauce
¼ cup cornstarch
1 16-ounce can bean sprouts

In saucepan cook onion in butter till tender but not brown. Add turkey, broth, celery, and water chestnuts; heat to boiling. Combine ⅓ cup water, soy sauce, and cornstarch; stir into turkey mixture. Cook and stir till mixture is thickened and bubbly.

Drain bean sprouts; add to mixture and heat through. Serve on hot rice sprinkled with toasted slivered almonds, if desired. Pass additional soy sauce. Makes 4 to 6 servings.

**CHORIZO**—A hot and peppery Spanish or Mexican pork sausage. (See also *Sausage*.)

**CHOU PASTE, CHOUX PASTE**—The French puff pastry dough from which cream puffs and éclairs are made. The round cream puff itself is known as a chou.

**CHOW CHOW**—A sweet pickle relish of chopped mixed vegetables strongly flavored with mustard. Both mustard seed and dry mustard may be used. The name originally referred to a Chinese relish of orange peel and ginger in a sweet syrup.

## Chow Chow

    7 large onions (4 cups)
    1 medium head cabbage (4 cups)
   10 green tomatoes (4 cups)
   12 green peppers (5 cups)
    6 sweet red peppers (1½ cups)
    ½ cup granulated pickling salt
    6 cups sugar
    2 tablespoons mustard seed
    1 tablespoon celery seed
    1½ teaspoons turmeric
    4 cups cider vinegar

Wash vegetables. Using coarse blade, grind onions, cabbage, green tomatoes, and peppers. Sprinkle with pickling salt; let mixture stand overnight. Rinse and drain.

Combine sugar, mustard seed, celery seed, turmeric, vinegar, and 2 cups water. Pour over vegetables. Bring to boil; boil gently 5 minutes.

Fill hot jars to within ½ inch of tops; adjust lids. Process jars in boiling water bath 5 minutes (start timing when the water returns to a full boil). Makes 9 pints.

**CHOWDER**—A thick soup, usually milk-based, and generally made with fish or shellfish. Chowder frequently contains bacon or salt pork and diced potatoes, while other vegetables may be included.

Chowder is said to have originated many years ago when French sailors, shipwrecked off the coast of New England, concocted a stew using the foods they had managed to salvage and clams dug from the sandy shore. The big iron kettle in which the stew was cooked was called a *chaudière*. It is easy to see how the Americanized name came into being.

Variations in chowder preparation have led to many arguments. New Englanders claim that fish or clam chowder is always made with milk as the base, salt pork as the fat, and diced potatoes as the thickener. Manhattan-style chowder, scorned in New England, contains tomatoes and other vegetables in a clear broth. In those parts of the country where fresh seafood is not readily available, the term chowder applies to a thick, creamy soup made with corn, potatoes, chicken, or cheese.

Whatever the ingredients, chowder is a meal in a bowl. Assorted crisp crackers and an easy fruit dessert complete a menu to nourish and satisfy. (See also *Soup.*)

## New England Clam Chowder

    2 dozen medium-size quahog clams
      *or* 2 7½-ounce cans clams
      *or* 1 pint fresh shucked clams
    ¼ pound salt pork, minced
    1½ cups water
    4 cups diced, peeled potatoes
    ½ cup chopped onion
    2 cups milk
    1 cup light cream
    3 tablespoons all-purpose flour
    1½ teaspoons salt
      Dash pepper

If using clams in shell, place them in large kettle; add 1 cup water. Cover and bring to boiling. Reduce heat; steam just till shells open, 5 to 10 minutes. Remove clams from shells.

Dice clams, reserving ½ cup clam liquor. Fry minced salt pork till crisp. Remove bits of pork; reserve. Add ½ cup clam liquor, water, potatoes, and onion to fat. Cook covered till potatoes are tender, 15 to 20 minutes.

Add clams, 1¾ *cups* milk, and the light cream. Blend remaining ¼ cup milk and flour; stir into chowder. Heat to boil; stir occasionally. Add seasonings and salt pork. Serves 6.

### *Seafood chowder by the bowlful*

New Englanders claim chowder must be→ seafood in a creamy soup, flavored with salt pork, and thickened with diced potatoes.

## Manhattan Clam Chowder

     2 dozen medium-size quahog clams
       *or* 2 7½-ounce cans clams
       *or* 1 pint fresh shucked clams
     3 slices bacon, finely diced
     1 cup finely diced celery
     1 cup chopped onion
     1 16-ounce can tomatoes, cut up
     2 cups diced, peeled potatoes
     1 cup finely diced carrots
    1½ teaspoons salt
     ¼ teaspoon dried thyme, crushed
       Dash pepper
     2 tablespoons all-purpose flour
     2 tablespoons water

If using clams in shell, place them in large kettle; add 1 cup water. Cover and bring to boiling. Reduce heat; steam just till shells open, 5 to 10 minutes. Remove clams from shells.

Dice clams finely. Strain liquor; reserve ½ cup. Partially cook bacon. Add celery and onion; cook till tender. Add 3 cups water and clam liquor. Add remaining vegetables and seasonings. Cover; simmer about 35 minutes. Blend flour with the 2 tablespoons cold water. Stir into chowder; cook and stir to boiling. Add clams; heat. Makes 6 to 8 servings.

## Clam Chowder au Vin

     2 cups diced, peeled potato
     ½ cup chopped onion
     ½ cup chopped celery
     ¼ teaspoon salt
     1 cup water
     1 10¾-ounce can condensed
       Manhattan-style clam chowder
     1 cup milk
     1 7½-ounce can minced clams,
       drained
     3 tablespoons dry white wine
     ½ cup whipping cream
     2 tablespoons snipped parsley

In large saucepan combine potatoes, onion, celery, salt, and water. Cook covered, till potatoes are tender, about 10 minutes; mash slightly. Add chowder, milk, clams, and wine. Heat but *do not boil*. Whip cream; stir into chowder. Season with salt and pepper. Sprinkle with parsley. Makes 4 servings.

## Seafood Chowder

*Inlanders can enjoy full-bodied chowder by using frozen fish fillets of haddock, cod, or halibut—*

     2 pounds fresh *or* frozen fish
       fillets (haddock, cod, etc.)*
     ¼ pound salt pork, diced
     1 cup chopped onion
     6 medium potatoes, peeled and
       cubed (about 4 cups)
     2 cups water
     2 teaspoons salt
     ¼ teaspoon pepper
     2 cups milk
     1 14½-ounce can evaporated
       milk (1⅔ cups)
     2 tablespoons all-purpose flour

Thaw frozen fillets. In large saucepan cook diced salt pork slowly till golden brown. Drain, reserving 1 tablespoon fat. Set aside cooked pork. Return the 1 tablespoon fat to saucepan. Add onion; cook till tender but not brown. Add potatoes and water. Add fillets; sprinkle with salt and pepper. Bring to boiling; cook over low heat till potatoes are tender and fish flakes easily when tested with fork. This will take 15 to 20 minutes.

With slotted spatula, remove fish. Break fish into bite-size pieces; return to saucepan. Combine milk and evaporated milk; gradually stir into flour till smooth; add to fish mixture. Add cooked salt pork and cook over low heat till mixture is heated through but do not allow chowder to boil. Makes 8 servings.

*\*Or* use 2 pounds halibut steaks; remove skin and bones carefully before breaking into pieces.

## Cheese Chowder

*Vegetable and cheese in a main dish soup—*

Cook ¼ cup finely chopped onion in 2 tablespoons butter or margarine till tender. Blend in ¼ cup all-purpose flour. Add 2 cups milk; one 13¾-ounce can chicken broth (1¾ cups, not condensed); ¼ cup *each* finely diced carrot and finely diced celery; and dash *each* salt and paprika. Cook and stir till thickened and bubbly. Reduce heat; add ½ cup cubed sharp process American cheese. Stir to melt cheese. Simmer 15 minutes. Makes 4 servings.

## Corned Beef Chowder

*Corned beef and "little" cabbages in creamy base—*

1 10½-ounce can condensed cream
  of potato soup
3 cups milk
1 10-ounce package frozen Brussels
  sprouts, thawed and cut up
  Dash pepper
1 12-ounce can corned beef,
  broken into pieces

In a large saucepan blend soup and *half* of the milk. Stir in Brussels sprouts and pepper. Bring to boiling, stirring occasionally. Reduce heat; simmer till sprouts are tender, 15 minutes. Add remaining milk and beef. Heat. Serves 4 or 5.

## Corn Chowder

5 slices bacon
2 cups diced potato
1 cup onion slices
1 16-ounce can whole kernel
  corn, undrained
1 10½-ounce can condensed cream
  of mushroom soup
2 cups milk
1 teaspoon salt
  Dash pepper
2 tablespoons all-purpose flour

Crisp-cook bacon; crumble. Reserve 2 table-spoons drippings. Cook potatoes and onion in 1 cup boiling salted water till tender. Do not drain. Stir in corn, mushroom soup, milk, salt, and pepper. Blend flour with reserved bacon drippings; add to soup mixture. Cook and stir till thick. Simmer 5 minutes. Stir often. Top with crumbled bacon. Serves 6 to 8.

**CHOW MEIN**—1. The Chinese term for fried noodles. 2. A stir-fried main dish consisting of meat and crisp vegetables served with fried noodles. Unlike American chow mein noodles, the Chinese versions are thin egg noodles cooked in water, then fried quickly. Often they are made into nestlike cakes and fried till brown and slightly crisp on the outside but still soft inside. (See also *Oriental Cookery.*)

## Pork Chow Mein

1 pound pork, cut in *thin* strips
3 tablespoons salad oil
3 cups thin, bias-cut celery
  slices
1 cup sliced onion
1 6-ounce can sliced mushrooms,
  drained
3 tablespoons cornstarch
1 10½-ounce can condensed beef
  broth
¼ cup soy sauce
1 16-ounce can bean sprouts,
  drained
1 5-ounce can water chestnuts,
  drained and sliced
  Cooked thin egg noodles* *or*
  heated chow mein noodles

Cook pork in *1 tablespoon* oil till done, about 10 minutes. Set aside. Cook celery, onion, and mushrooms in remaining oil till crisp-tender; stir often. Blend cornstarch and ¼ cup cold water; add broth and soy sauce. Stir into vegetables. Add meat, bean sprouts, and water chestnuts. Cook and stir till thick and bubbly. Serve over noodles. Serves 4 or 5.
*If desired, fry in small batches in 1 tablespoon oil over high heat until slightly crisp.

**CHOW MEIN NOODLES**—Crisp, fried noodles primarily served with chow mein in America, but also used as a crunchy topper for casseroles. When seasoned and toasted, the noodles make a tasty snack.

## Noodle Nibbles

3 tablespoons melted butter or
  margarine
2 teaspoons soy sauce
4 drops bottled hot pepper sauce
1 3-ounce can chow mein noodles
¼ teaspoon celery salt
  Dash onion powder

Combine melted butter or margarine, soy sauce, and hot pepper sauce; drizzle over noodles. Toss lightly. Sprinkle with celery salt and onion powder; toss. Spread on jelly-roll pan. Toast at 275° for 12 to 15 minutes. Makes 2½ cups.

# CHRISTMAS

*Food for holiday feasting and gift giving and the hospitality associated with the season.*

Fellowship and sharing of food keynote Christmas celebrations around the world. The religious and spiritual significance of this Christian holiday shines throughout the season and is enhanced by foods and customs which have become an important part of family observances. For many this significance is based on the heritage of a particular nationality or tradition.

In most homes Christmas celebrations last more than one day. Preparations often begin in late November or early December when fruitcakes are baked and the fragrance of freshly baked cookies fills the air. In many countries the holiday extends from Christmas Eve until January 6—the Twelve Days of Christmas.

In Sweden the celebration starts on December 13, Saint Lucia's Day. A daughter of the house, dressed in white and wearing a crown of lighted candles, begins the day by taking special bread or buns and coffee to her parents and other family members before they rise. In some towns the Lucia girl also visits the needy. Friends and neighbors exchange visits and hospitality during the day.

Many of the foods of the season originated in England. It was during Henry VIII's reign that fruitcakes and plum puddings were first served. By the seventeenth century mincemeat was being used in Christmas pie. Some of these were huge, weighing up to 100 pounds with a box-shaped crust to represent the manger of the Christ Child. Spices and fruits used in pies and puddings were considered reminders of the gifts of the Magi.

The custom of having a nativity scene in the home began in Italy. St. Francis of Assisi celebrated Mass in the forest, while, nearby, real people and live animals depicted the nativity. The idea of repeating the setting in miniature spread and much of the house-to-house calling on friends includes viewing the crèche and sampling a rich, sweet holiday bread, filled with fruit and decorated with almonds.

In Mexico, the *posada*, a reenactment of Mary and Joseph's search for lodging, combines spiritual devotion, hospitality, and a treat for the children. Families form a procession to the homes of friends. Their symbolic admittance is climaxed when the children, blindfolded, break the piñata, a decorated clay or paper-mache container filled with candy and trinkets.

In some German traditions, Belsnickel, a cranky character, watches children to make sure they are good every day until Christmas. If a child has been on his best behavior all day, he is rewarded the next morning by finding a little plate with a Christmas cookie placed on an outside kitchen window sill. If he's been naughty, the plate might be empty or contain a stone instead of a cookie.

## Yuletide entertaining

Holiday parties take many forms, but food is always an important element. An open house is perhaps the easiest way to entertain. Friends come by to exchange the season's greetings and sample an array of goodies presented for their enjoyment. Most of the foods are made in advance to free the hostess at serving time.

### *Sweets to say season's greetings*

← Jewel-topped Holiday Divinity and crunchy Peanut Brittle join Java Fudge and Peanut Butter Fudge as gifts from the kitchen.

The beverages offered at an open house are usually coffee, tea, and a cheery punch or Christmas beverage such as egg nog. All of these go well with fruitcake, cookies, and fancy breads. A hot punch is popular in cold climates. The Wassail bowl of Old English origin contains hot spiced fruit juice with or without wine. Glogg, another heated fruit and wine combination, comes from Scandinavia. Mixed drinks may be served, if desired.

## Rosy Wassail

In a large kettle combine 2 cups cranberry juice cocktail; one 6-ounce can frozen orange juice concentrate, thawed; 2 cups water; 1 tablespoon sugar; and ¼ teaspoon allspice. Bring *almost* to simmering. Add 3¼ cups dry sauterne; heat through, but do not boil. If desired, stir in a few drops red food coloring. Stud thick orange slices with whole cloves. Pour punch into preheated punch bowl; float orange slices atop. Makes 12 to 14 servings.

## Cranberry-Cherry Punch

Dissolve one 3-ounce package cherry-flavored gelatin in 1 cup boiling water. Stir in one 6-ounce can frozen lemonade concentrate. Add 3 cups cold water and one chilled 1-quart bottle cranberry juice cocktail. Pour over ice in punch bowl. Resting bottle on rim of bowl, slowly pour one chilled 28-ounce bottle ginger ale down the side; mix with up-and-down motion. Garnish with lime slices. Makes 25 servings.

Christmas dinner is one of the truly festive meals of the year. When the family gathering is large, roast turkey or goose, or perhaps a glazed ham, will provide ample servings. Smaller families might borrow from a Danish menu by serving Roast Duckling with Red Cabbage.

Accompaniments add a bountiful note to the dinner. Star-shaped molded salads are popular because they suit the season and can be made well ahead of time. If one or two kinds of potatoes plus a cooked vegetable—perhaps some buttered squash, creamed onions, or green beans amandine

## ❧MENU❧

### HOLIDAY FEAST
*Herring in Sour Cream*
*Roast Duckling*
*Red Cabbage     Parsley Buttered Potatoes*
*Cranberry-sauced Peaches*
*Hard Rolls     Celery and Carrot Sticks*
*Fruitcake*
*Beverage*

—are part of the menu, some hostesses prefer to pass a giant relish tray or crisp vegetables and pickles instead of a salad.

In some families plum pudding is a must for dessert. Others prefer mince pie, fruitcake, or a choice of cookies.

## Roast Duckling with Red Cabbage

      2 ducklings, 3 to 5 pounds each
      6 cups shredded red cabbage
    ¼ cup currant jelly
      2 tablespoons butter or margarine
      1 tablespoon vinegar
    ¾ teaspoon caraway seed
    ½ teaspoon salt

Prick skin of ducklings; place on rack in shallow roasting pan. Roast, uncovered, at 375° for 1½ to 2 hours. Increase temperature to 425°; roast an additional 15 minutes.

In large saucepan or kettle cook cabbage in boiling, salted water till tender, 10 minutes; drain well. Return to saucepan. In small saucepan combine remaining ingredients. Heat and stir till butter is melted. Pour over cabbage; toss and stir till cabbage is heated through. Serve with ducklings. Makes 4 to 5 servings.

### *Borrow a menu from Scandinavia*

Follow a Danish theme by serving Roast → Duckling with Red Cabbage. It is a festive choice for a small family gathering.

### ❊MENU❊

CHRISTMAS DINNER
*Fruit Cup*
*Currant Glazed Ham*
*Mashed Sweet Potatoes  Onions Au Gratin*
*Molded Ruby Red Salad*
*Cloverleaf Rolls          Relish Tray*
*Mincemeat Cake*
*Beverage*

## Festive breads

Among the joys of Christmas baking are the rich breads fragrant with spices and studded with bright bits of candied fruit or plump raisins. Before baking, the dough is braided or formed into special shapes befitting the season. While still warm from the oven, frosting is drizzled over the golden brown crust. Nuts, cherries, or colored sugars are used as trimmings.

## Lucia Braid

    2 packages active dry yeast
    5 to 5⅓ cups sifted all-purpose
      flour
    ½ teaspoon ground cardamom
    1⅓ cups milk
    ½ cup sugar
    ½ cup shortening
    1½ teaspoons salt
    2 eggs
      Confectioners' sugar glaze
      Walnut halves
      Red and green candied cherries

In large mixer bowl combine yeast, *3 cups* of the flour, and cardamom. Heat milk, sugar, shortening, and salt till warm; stir to melt shortening. Add to dry mixture in mixing bowl; add egg. Beat at low speed with electric mixer for ½ minute, scraping sides of bowl constantly. Beat 3 minutes at high speed. By hand, stir in enough of the flour to make a soft dough.

Turn dough out on well-floured surface. Knead till smooth and elastic, about 8 to 10 minutes. Place dough in lightly greased bowl; turning once to grease the surface. Cover, let rise in a warm place till doubled, about 2 hours. Punch down. Divide dough in half; cover and let rest 10 minutes. Divide each half in 4 parts.

Roll 3 parts of dough in 20-inch strands; braid. Carefully place braid around a greased, 6-ounce juice can standing upright on a greased baking sheet. Seal ends of dough together to form continuous braid. Divide 4th part of dough in half. Shape in two 20-inch strands and twist together. Place on top of large braid. Make second coffee cake with remaining pieces.

Let rise in warm place till doubled, about 1 hour. Bake at 350° till golden brown, about 25 minutes. Remove juice can.

## Currant-Glazed Ham

    14- to 16-pound fully cooked ham
      Whole cloves
    ¾ cup currant jelly
    ½ cup dark corn syrup
    ¼ teaspoon prepared horseradish
    ⅛ teaspoon dry mustard

Place ham, fat side up, on rack in shallow pan; insert meat thermometer. Heat at 325° till thermometer registers 130°, about 3 hours. About 30 minutes before ham is done, remove from oven; score diagonally, if desired. Stud with cloves. Return to oven; baste often with *Currant Glaze:* In saucepan combine jelly, corn syrup, horseradish, and dry mustard. Cook and stir over medium-low heat till blended.

## Molded Ruby Red Salad

*Avocado slices form a holiday wreath inside—*

Heat 2 cups cranberry-juice cocktail to boiling. Add two 3-ounce packages raspberry-flavored gelatin; stir to dissolve. Add one 8¾-ounce can pineapple tidbits, undrained; ½ cup port; and ½ cup water. Peel and slice 1 avocado; arrange slices in bottom of 5½-cup mold.

Pour enough gelatin mixture over avocado to cover; chill till almost set. Chill remaining cranberry mixture till partially set; fold in 1 cup diced peeled apple and ½ cup finely chopped celery. Pour over avocado layer. Chill till firm. Unmold. Makes 8 to 10 servings.

While braids are still warm, brush with Confectioners' Sugar Glaze. Decorate tops with nuts and candied cherries. Makes 2 coffee cakes.

*Confectioners' Sugar Glaze:* Add enough milk or cream to 2 cups sifted confectioners' sugar to make it spreading consistency. Add 1 teaspoon vanilla and dash salt; mix well.

## Jewel-Top Star Mold

*Trim bakes in pan like an upside-down cake—*

   1 package active dry yeast
 ¼ cup milk
   3 tablespoons shortening
   3 tablespoons granulated sugar
   1 teaspoon grated lemon peel
 ½ teaspoon salt
   1 egg
1½ cups sifted all-purpose flour

      • • •

   1 tablespoon butter or margarine, melted
   2 tablespoons brown sugar
   1 tablespoon light corn syrup
     Candied pineapple
     Candied cherries

Soften dry yeast in ¼ cup warm water. Heat milk and shortening till shortening melts; cool to lukewarm. Pour into mixing bowl. Stir in granulated sugar, lemon peel, and salt. Add egg and softened yeast. Add flour, ½ cup at a time, beating smooth after each addition. Cover and let rise till double. Stir down dough. Combine butter, brown sugar, and corn syrup; spread on bottom of 5½-cup star mold. Arrange fruit in mold to form pattern. Spoon dough carefully over fruit. Cover and let rise till double. Bake at 375° for 20 to 25 minutes. Cool 1 minute. Loosen sides and turn out onto rack. Cool.

Giving away holiday breads is part of the fun of baking. Sturdy cardboard, cut to fit and slipped under the bread, will support your gift as you carry it to a neighbor or friend. A new bread board or baking sheet tucked under the loaf also can be a part of the gift. Clear plastic wrap used as a covering material serves two purposes. It lets the gaily-decorated loaf show through as it protects the bread.

# Gift-worthy candies

An assortment of Christmas candies makes a dandy holiday remembrance. Show off your talents as a candymaker by offering candies with a variety of interesting textures and flavors. A good selection should include some that contain combinations of nuts, fruit, or coconut and others that are plain. In peanut brittles or other nut brittles, the nuts are essential both for flavor and crunch. But, in many candies the ingredients can be mixed or matched to suit your fancy.

Velvety-smooth chocolate fudge is an all-time favorite, but this year why not treat your friends to Java Fudge or Peanut Butter Fudge. Let taffy or caramels provide a delightful contrast in chewiness. Creamy white divinity can be dressed up with candied-fruit jewels.

The container for these masterpieces may be as simple as a brightly papered box, or as fancy as a candy dish or brandy snifter tied with a saucy red bow.

## Peanut Butter Fudge

In a large, warm bowl combine 1 pint marshmallow creme, 1 cup chunk-style peanut butter, and 1 teaspoon vanilla. In a heavy saucepan combine 2 cups sugar and ⅔ cup milk. Cook sugar mixture to soft ball stage, or till candy thermometer registers 234°. Pour over peanut butter mixture. Blend well. Spread in buttered 8- or 9-inch square pan. Cool; cut in squares.

## Java Fudge

In heavy 3-quart saucepan combine 3 cups sugar, 4 teaspoons instant coffee powder, and dash salt. Stir in 1 cup milk, ½ cup light cream, and 2 tablespoons light corn syrup. Bring to boiling stirring constantly. Continue boiling over medium heat without stirring, till candy thermometer registers 234°. Remove from heat; add 3 tablespoons butter or margarine and 1 teaspoon vanilla. *Do not stir.* Cool to 110°.

Beat till mixture begins to thicken and starts to lose its gloss. Quickly stir in ¼ cup chopped walnuts. Pour into buttered 8-inch pan. Cool; cut into squares. Makes 1½ pounds.

## Molasses Taffy

Butter sides of heavy 2-quart saucepan. In it combine 2 cups granulated sugar, 1 cup light molasses, and ⅓ cup water. Heat slowly stirring constantly till sugar dissolves. Bring mixture to boiling; add 2 teaspoons vinegar. Cook to soft-crack stage (268°).

Remove from heat; add 2 tablespoons butter. Sift in ½ teaspoon soda; stir to mix. Pour into buttered 15½x10½x1-inch pan. Cool till comfortable to handle. Butter hands; gather taffy into ball and pull with fingertips. When light taffy color and hard to pull, cut into fourths. Pull each piece into long strand about ½ inch thick. With buttered scissors cut in bite-size pieces; wrap in waxed paper. Makes 1¼ pounds.

## Peanut Brittle

  2 cups sugar
  1 cup light corn syrup
  1 cup water
  2 cups raw Spanish or Virginia*
       peanuts
  ½ teaspoon salt
  1 teaspoon butter or margarine
  ½ teaspoon soda

Combine sugar, syrup, and water in heavy skillet. Cook slowly, stirring till sugar dissolves. Cook to soft-ball stage (234°). Add peanuts and salt. Cook to hard-crack stage (290°), stirring constantly. (Remove candy from heat while testing.) Add butter and soda; stir quickly to blend. (Mixture will bubble.) Pour at once onto 2 well-buttered 15½x10½x1-inch jelly roll pans. Tilt pans slightly to allow candy to spread in thin layer. Break in pieces when cold. Makes about 1½ pounds candy.

*Blanch peanuts in boiling water. Let stand 3 minutes; run under cold water; peel.

### *Pass Christmas cookies and cake*

← Decorated Family-Style Sugar Cookies and Gingerbreadmen, Chocolate Spritz, Orange-Date Bars, and Mint-Topped Brownies join Cranberry-Cherry Punch and triple-layered Mincemeat Cake as holiday refreshments. (See *Gingerbread* for Gingerbreadmen.)

## Holiday Divinity

  ½ cup light corn syrup
  2½ cups sugar
  ¼ teaspoon salt
  ½ cup water
  2 egg whites
  1 teaspoon vanilla
  1 cup coarsely chopped walnuts
  ¼ cup chopped candied cherries
  ¼ cup chopped candied pineapple

In saucepan mix corn syrup, sugar, salt, and water. Cook, stirring, till sugar is dissolved. Continue cooking, without stirring, till candy thermometer registers 248° or till firm-ball stage. Beat egg whites till stiff peaks form. Gradually pour about *half* the syrup over whites, beating constantly with electric mixer. Then cook remainder of syrup till thermometer registers 272° or till soft-crack stage. Slowly beat into first mixture. Add vanilla. Beat till mixture holds its shape. If necessary, allow mixture to stand about 5 minutes to stiffen; stir occasionally. Add nuts and fruits. Drop by teaspoonfuls onto waxed paper. Makes 4 dozen.

# Cookies with trimmings

Cookie baking for the holidays is a labor of love. Soft bars, crisp rolled cookies, and tender spritz head the list of favorites. Frostings and trims add to the fun especially when the children help.

Sugar cookies are perhaps the most versatile because each shape and decoration yields a different looking cookie. Use fancy cutters, or make your own pattern out of heavy paper and trace the design onto the rolled dough. To turn sugar cookies into Christmas ornaments, simply make a tiny hole near the top of each cookie before it goes into the oven. The point of a skewer or wooden pick will do the job nicely. When baked, the opening is just right for stringing the ornament with twine or yarn.

Many cookies that are filled with candied fruit and spices stay moist throughout the season's entertaining if stored in tightly covered containers or frozen. Brandy Balls and Cherry-Almond Balls are good keepers—that is if hungry nibblers don't get into the cookie jar first.

## Family-Style Sugar Cookies

2 cups sifted all-purpose flour
¾ cup sugar
1 teaspoon baking powder
¼ teaspoon salt
  Dash nutmeg
½ cup shortening
1 beaten egg
⅓ cup milk
½ teaspoon vanilla

Sift together flour, sugar, baking powder, salt, and nutmeg. Using pastry blender, cut in shortening till like fine crumbs. Combine egg, milk, and vanilla. Stir into flour-shortening mixture. Blend well. On floured surface roll to ⅛-inch thickness for crisp cookies or ¼-inch for softer cookies. Cut with cutters. Sprinkle with sugar *or* leave plain if cookies are to be frosted. Bake on lightly greased cookie sheets at 375° for 7 to 8 minutes for thin cookies and 11 to 12 minutes for thicker cookies. Makes 2 dozen cookies, ⅛ inch thick *or* 1½ dozen ¼ inch thick.

## Fruitcake Cookies

¼ cup butter or margarine
¾ cup brown sugar
1 egg
¼ cup evaporated milk
1 teaspoon lemon juice

• • •

1 cup sifted all-purpose flour
¼ teaspoon baking soda
¼ teaspoon salt
½ teaspoon ground cinnamon
½ teaspoon ground cloves
½ teaspoon ground allspice
  Dash ground nutmeg
1 cup chopped mixed candied fruits
  and peels
1 cup chopped pecans
¾ cup raisins

Cream butter and sugar till fluffy; beat in egg. Combine milk and lemon juice; gradually add to creamed mixture. Reserve ¼ cup flour. Sift remaining flour with soda, salt, and spices; stir into creamed mixture. Mix reserved flour with fruits and pecans; blend into dough. Drop by teaspoon on lightly greased cookie sheet. Bake at 375° for 10 to 12 minutes. Makes 60.

## Chocolate Spritz

1½ cups butter or margarine
1 cup sugar
2 ounces unsweetened chocolate,
  melted
1 egg
1 teaspoon vanilla
½ teaspoon almond extract
4 cups sifted all-purpose flour
1 teaspoon baking powder

In large mixer bowl thoroughly cream butter and sugar; add melted chocolate, egg, vanilla, and almond extract. Beat well.

Sift together flour and baking powder. Add to creamed mixture; mix till smooth. Do not chill. Force dough through cookie press, forming various shapes, on greased cookie sheet. Bake at 400° 8 to 10 minutes. Cool. Decorate.

## Snowy Cinnamon Stars

Mix ⅔ cup sugar, 1 teaspoon ground cinnamon, and ½ teaspoon grated lemon peel. Beat 2 egg whites till soft peaks form. Gradually add sugar mixture. Beat till very stiff peaks form. Fold in 1¾ cups ground almonds. Chill.

On lightly floured surface, roll dough ⅛ inch thick. Cut with 2½-inch star cutter. Place on well-greased cookie sheet. Frost to points with Meringue. Trim with silver candies. Bake at 325° for 12 to 15 minutes; remove from sheet at once. Cool on rack. Makes about 3 dozen.

*Meringue:* Beat 1 egg white till soft peaks form. Gradually add 1 cup sifted confectioners' sugar, beating after each addition. Continue beating till stiff peaks form. Frost star cookies with meringue before baking.

## Date-Orange Bars

Cream ¼ cup butter and ½ cup brown sugar till fluffy. Add 1 egg and 1 teaspoon grated orange peel; beat well. Sift together 1 cup sifted all-purpose flour, ½ teaspoon baking powder, and ½ teaspoon soda; add to creamed mixture. Stir in ¼ cup milk, ¼ cup orange juice, ½ cup chopped walnuts, and ½ cup chopped dates.

Spread in greased 11x7x1½-inch pan. Bake at 350° for 25 minutes. Cool; sprinkle with confectioners' sugar. Makes 24.

## Brandy Balls

2½ cups finely crushed vanilla
     wafers (about 60 wafers)
  1 cup sifted confectioners' sugar
  2 tablespoons unsweetened cocoa
     powder
  ½ cup finely chopped walnuts
  ¼ cup brandy
  ¼ cup light corn syrup

Combine wafer crumbs, confectioners' sugar, cocoa powder, and nuts. Stir in brandy and corn syrup. Add a little water (about 1¼ teaspoons) if necessary to form mixture into ¾-inch balls. Roll in granulated sugar. Store in tightly covered container. Makes 4 dozen.

## Cherry-Almond Balls

  ¾ cup butter or margarine
  ⅓ cup sifted confectioners' sugar
  1 teaspoon vanilla
  ¼ teaspoon salt
  2 cups sifted all-purpose flour
  ½ cup finely chopped almonds
     Whole candied cherries (about
     60 cherries)

Cream together butter, sugar, vanilla, and salt till fluffy. Add flour and almonds; mix well. Wrap a teaspoonful of dough around each cherry. Place on baking sheet. Bake at 325° for 20 minutes. Cool slightly. Roll in sifted confectioners' sugar. Makes about 5 dozen.

## Mint-Frosted Brownies

Thoroughly cream ½ cup butter or margarine, 1 cup sugar, and 1 teaspoon vanilla. Add 2 eggs and beat well. Blend in 2 ounces unsweetened chocolate, melted. Stir in ½ cup sifted all-purpose flour and ½ cup chopped nuts. Bake in greased 8x8x2-inch pan at 350° for 30 to 35 minutes. Cool; frost with Mint Frosting.

*Mint Frosting:* Cream 3 tablespoons soft butter, ½ teaspoon peppermint extract, and dash salt. Gradually add 1 cup sifted confectioners' sugar, creaming till light and fluffy. Add 2 tablespoons milk or cream and another cup sifted confectioners' sugar. Beat till smooth. Tint with few drops red or green food coloring.

# Traditional desserts

Leading contenders in many countries for this title are fruitcake, plum pudding, or desserts made with mincemeat. Showy desserts such as a Lithuanian Strawberry Torte are favored, too.

Fruitcake takes special honors in the make-ahead category because many varieties can be baked several weeks in advance and stored to mellow before slicing. The fruitcake is wrapped in brandy-soaked cheesecloth and placed in a canister with a snug-fitting lid. If you prefer, wedges of apple changed periodically during storage may replace the moistened cheesecloth. Should you be tardy in baking your fruitcake, last-minute versions like this Whole Nut Fruitcake are delicious, too.

## Whole Nut Fruitcake

Sift together 1 cup sifted all-purpose flour, 1 teaspoon baking powder, and ⅛ teaspoon salt. Separate 4 eggs. Beat yolks till thick. Add 1 cup sugar to egg yolks, beating constantly. Add ¼ cup milk and sifted dry ingredients. Beat egg whites till stiff peaks form. Fold beaten egg whites into the batter.

In a large bowl, mix 16 ounces pitted dates with 8 ounces *each* candied pineapple, whole candied cherries, mixed candied fruit and peels, pecan halves, walnut halves, and whole Brazil nuts. Add batter and mix well. Spoon fruitcake mixture into two well-greased and floured 9x5x 3-inch pans. Bake at 325° for 1½ hours. Cool; remove fruitcake from pans. When cold, store fruitcake in an airtight container.

Christmas plum pudding can be made ahead and reheated, but many hostesses will serve it steaming hot from the mold. For a spectacular touch, it may be served aflame. Warmed brandy, ignited and quickly poured over the pudding, will wreathe it in flame. Another way to flame the plum pudding is to saturate sugar cubes with brandy or lemon extract, arrange them around the base of the pudding and ignite the cubes. Flamed or not, hard sauce or foamy sauce are accompaniments to pass with this traditional dessert.

## English Plum Pudding

    1 cup all-purpose flour
    1 teaspoon baking soda
    1 teaspoon salt
    1 teaspoon ground cinnamon
    ¾ teaspoon ground mace
    ¼ teaspoon ground nutmeg
    8 ounces raisins (1½ cups)
    8 ounces currants (1½ cups)
    4 ounces mixed candied fruits
        and peels (½ cup)
    ½ cup chopped walnuts
    2 cups coarse soft bread
        crumbs (4 slices)
    4 ounces ground suet (1½ cups)
    1 cup brown sugar
    2 beaten eggs
    ¼ cup currant jelly
    ⅓ cup brandy
        Hard Sauce

Sift together flour, soda, salt, and spices. Stir in fruits, nuts, and bread crumbs. Combine suet, sugar, eggs, jelly, and brandy. Blend into flour-fruit mixture. Pour into two well-greased 1-quart molds; cover tightly. Steam 3 to 3½ hours. Let stand 5 to 10 minutes; unmold. Serve warm with Hard Sauce.

*Hard Sauce:* Thoroughly cream ½ cup butter with 2 cups sifted confectioners' sugar. Beat in 1 tablespoon brandy. Chill in mold or bowl; unmold before serving. *Or* use pastry tube to make individual decorations; chill till firm.

## Mincemeat Cake

Cream together 1½ cups sugar and ½ cup shortening. Add 3 eggs and 1 teaspoon vanilla; beat till fluffy. Sift together 2½ cups sifted all-purpose flour, 2 teaspoons baking powder, 1 teaspoon baking soda, and 1 teaspoon salt. Add alternately with 1 cup milk to sugar mixture, beating thoroughly after each addition. Fold in 1½ cups prepared mincemeat.

Divide batter evenly among 3 greased and floured 9-inch round cake pans. Bake at 350° for 25 to 30 minutes. Cool 10 minutes. Remove from pans and fill with Vanilla Nut Filling. Drizzle with a confectioners' sugar glaze.

*Vanilla Nut Filling:* Make one 3-ounce package regular vanilla pudding mix following label. Cool; stir in ¼ cup chopped pecans.

## Strawberry Torte

    1 cup butter or margarine,
        softened
    1 cup sugar
    6 egg yolks
    2 cups sifted cake flour
    ½ teaspoon baking powder
    ½ teaspoon salt
    6 egg whites
    ¾ cup sugar
    3 cups whipping cream
    1 tablespoon sugar
    1 teaspoon vanilla
    ½ cup currant jelly
    1 cup coarsely chopped pecans
    1 12-ounce jar strawberry
        preserves (1 cup)

In large mixer bowl, cream together butter or margarine and the 1 cup sugar till very light and fluffy. Add egg yolks, one at a time, beating well after each addition. Beat till very fluffy and smooth, about 5 minutes.

Sift together cake flour, baking powder, and salt; stir into creamed mixture. Beat egg whites until soft peaks form; gradually add the ¾ cup sugar, beating to stiff peaks. Fold egg whites into batter. Pour batter into 3 lightly greased 9x1½-inch round layer cake pans. Bake at 350° for 30 to 35 minutes. Cool.

*To assemble:* Whip cream with the 1 tablespoon sugar and the vanilla. Place one layer of cake on serving plate; spread with currant jelly and *1 cup* of the whipped cream. Sprinkle with *2 tablespoons* of the chopped pecans.

Gently place second layer on cake. Spread top with ⅔ *cup* of the strawberry preserves and *another 1 cup* whipped cream. Sprinkle with *2 tablespoons* chopped pecans.

Gently add third cake layer. Frost top and sides with remaining 1½ cups whipped cream and coat sides with the remaining ¾ cup pecans. Using the tip of a spoon, dot whipped cream-topped cake with remaining ⅓ cup of the strawberry preserves.

### A holiday spectacular

Ruby-red jam made from summer's bright →
berries sparkles atop this Strawberry Torte,
a Christmas tradition from Lithuania.

This melon has been labeled Christmas or Santa Claus because it ripens in storage and can then be enjoyed during the holidays.

**CHRISTMAS MELON**—A large, oblong variety of winter melon (also called Santa Claus melon) identified by its mottled green and gold surface.

Christmas melons usually weigh from six to nine pounds. The flesh is a thick, firm, and juicy yellowish green similar to honeydew melon. A mild and slightly sweet flavor is characteristic in spite of its pungent aroma. (See also *Melon*.)

**CHRISTMAS PUDDING**—Another term for the steamed dessert plum pudding traditionally served in England at Christmas. (See *Christmas, Plum Pudding* for additional information.)

**CHUB**—A small, freshwater fish of the carp family. Several varieties of chubs inhabit the Great Lakes. Soft texture and mild flavor, much like whitefish, make chubs suitable for smoking.

**CHUCK**—The shoulder cut of a beef carcass. Well-known retail cuts of chuck include boneless chuck pot roast, blade pot roast, and arm pot roast, all of which may simply be labeled "chuck roast." Except for the chuck cut called "petite steak," all require slow cooking in some liquid and must be braised. (See also *Beef*.)

## Polynesian Beef Roast

  1  3- to 4-pound beef chuck roast
  1  large onion, sliced
  1  cup pineapple juice
 ¼  cup soy sauce
1½  teaspoons ground ginger
  1  cup diagonally sliced celery
  4  carrots, cut in 3- to 4-inch strips
 ½  pound spinach, cleaned and stems removed *or* 10-ounce package frozen spinach, thawed
  2  cups fresh mushrooms, sliced
  2  tablespoons cornstarch

In shallow baking dish cover meat with onion. Combine pineapple juice, soy sauce, ginger, and ¼ teaspoon salt. Pour over meat. Marinate 1 hour at room temperature, turning meat once.

Place meat and onions in Dutch oven. Pour pineapple mixture over. Cover; simmer till meat is tender, about 2 to 2½ hours. Add celery and carrots. Sprinkle vegetables with salt; bring to boiling; then simmer 20 minutes.

Arrange spinach and mushrooms atop meat. Simmer till spinach is wilted and other vegetables are crisp-tender, about 10 minutes. Remove meat and vegetables to platter; keep hot. Skim fat from meat juices. Blend together ¼ cup cold water and cornstarch. Stir into juices; cook and stir till thick and bubbly. Serves 6 to 8.

**CHURN**—1. The equipment in which milk or cream is agitated to separate the milk fat in a solid mass from the liquid, thereby making butter. 2. The action by which milk or cream fat is separated. (See also *Butter*.)

**CHUTNEY**—An exotic relish that originated in India and is the principal accompanying condiment for curry and other highly spiced dishes. Chutneys may be puréed or chopped mixtures.

Their pastelike consistency identifies chutneys of India which are usually made fresh daily. The flavors are either sweet (based on ripe fruit) or tart (based on vegetables) and almost always are hot. The commercially bottled Indian chutneys are often based on mangoes and may contain tamarinds, raisins, ginger, and other spices. "Major Grey's" chutney, readily

Baked Chutney Pears play a dual role as meat accompaniment and garnish when served on a platter with roast lamb or ham.

available in the United States, is not a brand name but a specific type of chutney made with green mangoes and marketed by a number of manufacturers.

In American versions of chutney, the fruit is left in rather large pieces with a definite shape. These chutneys are richly spiced, but not always hot, and often hint of the sweet-sour. Traditional homemade relishes called chutneys may include mixtures of ripe or green tomatoes, plums, apricots, pumpkin, apples, or peaches.

Chutneys, puréed or chopped, are delicious accompaniments for cold meats and cheeses, as well as curries. As recipe ingredients or garnishes, chutneys add a distinctive flavor. (See *Curry, Indian Cookery* for additional information.)

## Currant Chutney

Mix ½ cup chutney, cut up; ½ cup red currant jelly, 3 tablespoons dried currants, and 2 tablespoons dry white wine. Serve with curries.

## Baked Chutney Pears

  1 16-ounce can pear halves, drained
  1 tablespoon butter or margarine, melted
  3 tablespoons chutney

Place drained pears, cut side up, on rack in baking dish. Brush with butter. Spoon about ½ tablespoon chutney in the center of each pear half. Bake at 325° for 15 minutes, or till hot. Serve with ham or lamb. Makes 6 servings.

## Chutney Cheddar Spread

  1 cup shredded natural Cheddar cheese
  ¼ cup chopped chutney
  2 tablespoons butter or margarine
  1 teaspoon instant minced onion
  ¼ teaspoon Worcestershire sauce
     Dash bottled hot pepper sauce
     Assorted crackers

Combine first 6 ingredients in small mixer bowl. Beat with electric mixer till fluffy. Serve with assorted crackers. Makes ⅔ cup.

## Orange Chutney Chops

  4 loin pork chops, ¾ inch thick
  ¼ cup water
     • • •
  ½ cup chopped chutney
  ¼ cup sugar
  ¼ cup water
  2 tablespoons lemon juice
  1 medium orange

In heavy skillet brown pork chops well on both sides over medium heat; pour off excess fat. Add the first ¼ cup water; cover and simmer till tender, about 45 minutes. Combine chutney, sugar, the remaining water, and lemon juice. Peel orange and cut in four ½-inch slices. Place over chops. Pour chutney mixture over.

Continue cooking chops, spooning liquid over occasionally, till liquid becomes slightly syrupy, about 10 to 15 minutes. Arrange the chops on a serving platter. Stir pan juices and pour over the chops. Makes 4 servings.

**CIDER**—A fermented and/or sweet beverage made from the juice extracted from apples. France is the largest producer of fermented cider; extensive production is also found in England. Although most kinds of apples can be used, special varieties are required for high-quality cider.

Cider has been commercially important in France for many years. Likewise, English cider is made by highly developed processes in factories, although it was farm oriented until the twentieth century.

In 1908, the French began regulating the labeling of cider: no beverage may be identified as cider unless it is produced entirely from fermented apple juice, or from a mixture of fermented apple and pear juices with or without the addition of water. *Cidre pur juice* is limited to cider made without the addition of water. *Cidre* applies only to a beverage which contains a certain amount of dry extract, ash, and at least 3.5 percent by volume of alcohol. Cider containing a smaller amount of alcohol, extract, and ash is labeled *petite cidre*. English regulations, less strict, forbid the label of cider on any beverage which does not have fermented apple juice as its base.

Since the United States does not produce an alcoholic cider in significant quantity, these European standards do not apply in America. In fact, the use of the term has caused much confusion. American processors label their apple juice products "cider," "apple cider," or "sweet cider;" their choice is determined by the most popular market term. Usually, all three terms refer to pure, unfermented apple juice.

Country cider, produced on local farms and generally sold at roadside stands, may be fermented or partially fermented. Partially fermented cider to which benzoate of soda has been added, may also be labeled as sweet cider, due to its low alcoholic content. Country cider that has been allowed to ferment completely, thus having a much higher alcoholic content, is known as hard cider. Hard cider and imported cider are sometimes available in retail liquor stores.

Hard cider or imported cider are often served alone, much the same as beer is served. Apple cider (unfermented) is popular as a beverage during the fall season. In addition to being used in hot and cold drinks or punches, apple cider lends itself to cooking, for basting and barbecue sauces, and as part of the liquid in gelled salads or baked products. (See also *Apple*.)

## American Hot Mulled Apple Cider

  ½ cup brown sugar
  1 teaspoon whole allspice
  1 teaspoon whole cloves
  ¼ teaspoon salt
     Dash ground nutmeg
  3 inches stick cinnamon
  2 quarts apple cider
     Orange wedges
     Whole cloves

Combine first 7 ingredients in large saucepan. Bring to boiling. Cover; simmer 20 minutes. Strain to remove spices. Serve in mugs with clove-studded orange wedges. Makes 8 servings.

## Apple Cider Snap

In saucepan combine 1 quart apple cider *or* apple juice and 2 tablespoons red cinnamon candies. Heat and stir till candies dissolve and cider is hot. Serve in mugs with apple-slice floaters. Makes 6 to 8 servings.

**CIDER VINEGAR**—A sour liquid made by controlled fermentation of apple cider, used as a flavoring agent and as a food preservative. Light golden brown, it has a faint taste of apple. Its acidity is due primarily to acetic acid produced during fermentation. Its total acidity usually ranges from four to six percent. Cider vinegar is the vinegar most often preferred in the United States. (See also *Vinegar*.)

## *Golden, spicy refreshment*

Swirl American Hot Mulled Apple Cider→ with cinnamon stick and add clove-studded orange wedge. Serve in a king-sized mug.

**CINNAMON**—A sweet-pungent spice derived from the dried bark of a tree in the evergreen family. Cinnamon is one of the oldest spices, dating back to 2700 B.C. It has been used for centuries not only to flavor food, but also as a medicine, a perfume ingredient, and an aromatic substance burned as incense. The Greeks made offerings of cinnamon boughs to Apollo; Romans luxuriated in cinnamon-scented baths; and cinnamon-oil candles, rare and costly, were used in medieval churches.

***How cinnamon is produced:*** Although several varieties of cinnamon-producing trees are grown, the processing method is similar for all. At harvest, the dried bark is slit and stripped off both the trunk and branches. It is then rolled into long, slender "quills," known as cinnamon sticks. The quills, sometimes as long as 30 inches, are exported for grinding.

***Types of cinnamon:*** Trees producing cinnamon are in the *Cinnamomum* family. Most of the cinnamon used in the United States is of the *cassia* variety which is coarse, dark, and pungent. The three types of cassia cinnamon on the American market are Saigon cinnamon, Korintje cinnamon, and Padang (Batavia) cinnamon. Saigon cinnamon, imported from South Vietnam, is judged best in flavor because the bark contains a high percentage of essential oil. Korintje and Padang cinnamon are both grown on the island of Sumatra. Korintje rates higher than Padang for its more intense color and flavor.

Ceylon cinnamon, another variety, is much lighter in color, flavor, and aroma than the cassia cinnamons. Although some Ceylon cinnamon is imported here, most of it is reexported to Mexico where it is a popular ingredient in many foods.

***How to store:*** The aroma and flavor of cinnamon are retained much longer in stick form than in ground form. Thus, since ground cinnamon weakens with storage, don't buy it in great quantities—buy small amounts of fresh cinnamon periodically. Cinnamon is best stored in a cool, dry place—excessive heat may weaken the flavor and high humidity causes caking.

***How to use:*** One of the most popular spices, cinnamon is often used in breads, salads, desserts, beverages, and some meat dishes. Ground cinnamon emits flavor more readily than stick cinnamon since grinding cuts through the cell walls, exposing the flavor-bearing oils. Stick cinnamon is most often used for spicing clear liquids that might be clouded by ground cinnamon. Cinnamon sticks also serve as handy, flavorful stirrers for hot beverages. (See also *Spice.*)

## Cinnamon-Raisin Bars

½ cup butter or margarine
1 cup brown sugar
1½ cups sifted all-purpose flour
½ teaspoon baking soda
1½ cups quick-cooking rolled oats
Raisin Filling
Cinnamon Icing

Cream butter and sugar. Sift together flour, soda, and ½ teaspoon salt; stir into creamed mixture. Add oats and 1 tablespoon water. Mix till crumbly. Firmly pat *half* the mixture in greased 13x9x2-inch baking dish. Spread with Raisin Filling. Mix remaining crumbs and 1 tablespoon water; spoon over filling. Pat smooth. Bake at 350° for 35 minutes. Cool. Drizzle with Cinnamon Icing. Makes 30.

*Raisin Filling:* In saucepan combine ¼ cup granulated sugar and 1 tablespoon cornstarch. Stir in 1 cup water and 2 cups seedless raisins. Cook and stir till thick and bubbly.

*Cinnamon Icing:* Mix 1 cup sifted confectioners' sugar with ¼ teaspoon ground cinnamon. Stir in enough milk, about 1 tablespoon, for drizzling consistency.

**CINNAMON SUGAR**—A mixture of ground cinnamon and granulated sugar, used as a topping for fruit or to make cinnamon toast. Easily blended at home, it is available on the market in a shaker-top jar.

**CIOPPINO** (*chuh pē′ nō*)—A fish stew which supposedly originated in California. Although many variations exist, it is made with both fish and shellfish, tomatoes, onion, wine, and seasonings.

## Cioppino

   ¼ cup finely chopped onion
   3 cloves garlic, minced
   1 tablespoon snipped parsley
   ¼ cup olive oil
   1 28-ounce can tomatoes
   2 8-ounce cans tomato sauce
   ½ teaspoon dried oregano leaves,
      crushed
   ½ teaspoon dried marjoram leaves,
      crushed
   ½ cup dry sherry
   2 12-ounce uncooked rock-lobster
      tails, cut in serving pieces,
      shell and all
1½ pounds whitefish (sole, haddock,
      halibut, *or* cod), cut up
   ⅔ pound raw cleaned shrimp
      (1 pound in shell)
   2 dozen clams in shell* *or* 3
      7½-ounce cans minced
      clams, drained

In Dutch oven cook onion, garlic, and parsley in hot oil till onion is tender. Add tomatoes, next 3 ingredients, 1½ cups water, 1 teaspoon salt, and dash pepper. Cover; bring to boiling. Reduce heat; simmer, uncovered, for 20 minutes. Add sherry; simmer 10 minutes longer.

Stir in remaining ingredients, adding drained clams last. Cover tightly; bring to boiling. Reduce heat; cook slowly for 15 minutes. (Clam shells will pop open during cooking.) Serve in heated soup bowls. Makes 6 servings.

*To prepare clams in shells:* Scrub shells. Allow clams to stand in cold salted water (⅓ cup salt to 1 gallon water) for 15 minutes. Repeat twice. Refrigerate till ready to use.

**CISCO** *(sis′ kō)*—A species of whitefish native to the Great Lakes of Canada and the United States. It is sold smoked, then skinned and flaked for use in creamed fish dishes or salads. (See also *Fish.*)

**CITRIC ACID**—An acid which appears naturally in citrus fruits, currants, pineapples, pears, and many berries. It has a pleasant, sour taste. Extracted from lime or lemon juice, it is used commercially as a flavoring agent in a wide variety of foods and carbonated beverages.

**CITRON**—A citrus fruit grown chiefly for its thick peel which is candied and used as a baking ingredient, especially in fruitcakes. It resembles a lemon but is longer and yellow green in color. Citron is grown primarily in Mediterranean countries and the West Indies.

Depending upon the variety of citron, the pulp may be acid or sweet. In either case, the pulp is used only for by-products; the peel from either type is the main product. The peel is first soaked in brine or seawater to remove the bitter oil and to intensify the flavor. It is then candied in sugar before marketing.

Candied citron is available halved or diced in various sized jars or sold in bulk. It should be moist and slightly sticky; if hard and crystallized, it has been stored too long. (See also *Citrus Fruit.*)

## Fruit Bread

   2 cups sifted all-purpose flour
   ¾ cup sugar
   3 teaspoons baking powder
   ½ teaspoon salt
   2 beaten eggs
   1 cup milk
   3 tablespoons salad oil
   ¼ cup diced candied citron
   ¼ cup dried currants
   2 tablespoons finely diced
      candied cherries
   2 tablespoons diced candied
      lemon peel
   ½ cup chopped walnuts

Sift together first 4 ingredients. Combine eggs, milk, and salad oil; add to flour mixture, beating well (about ½ minute). Stir in fruits and nuts. Turn into greased 9x5x3-inch loaf pan. Bake at 350° about 50 minutes. Remove from pan; cool on rack. Wrap and store overnight.

**CITRON MELON**—A member of the watermelon family, it is inedible raw. Much harder than the popular watermelon, it has a white flesh and red seeds. Sometimes known as preserving melon, the flesh of the melon is candied with sugar and used in making conserves.

# CITRUS FRUIT

*How to add tangy flavor and vivid color to*
*any meal with these vitamin-rich fruits.*

Tart and fresh-flavored fruits of citrus trees comprise a large group known as citrus fruit, the most familiar being the orange, lemon, lime, grapefruit, kumquat, citron, tangerine, mandarin, and tangelo.

These fruits have a long, intriguing history. They originated in the tropical regions of Asia and from there were taken into the Mediterranean area. In the twelfth century, Crusaders returning from the Holy Lands introduced many varieties of citrus fruits to their European countries.

Citrus fruits became popular because of their nutritive value as well as their taste appeal. These fruits, especially rich in vitamin C (ascorbic acid), were found to prevent the disease scurvy. The British Navy provided their sailors with limes during long voyages to prevent the disease. This is the origin of the nickname "limey" for British seamen. These seamen were particularly fond of the limes when the juice was mixed with gin.

Citrus fruits were brought to America by Columbus. On his second voyage, from 1493 to 1496, citrus trees were planted in Haiti. More were planted in the area around St. Augustine, Florida, in 1565.

During the California Gold Rush, many prospectors developed scurvy because of a lack of fresh fruit. Lemons, very much in demand, sold for as much as one dollar each. Commercial planting of citrus trees in California began at this time, marking the advent of California's citrus industry.

### Exotic citrus fruit

← Eat the tangelo in segments or use its juice and peel for heavenly Tangelo Chiffon Pie. Tangerine can be substituted in the pie.

The use of citrus fruits has grown steadily in America. In fact, consumption has more than tripled since 1900. The average American eats 80 to 90 pounds of citrus fruit products each year—oranges account for about two-thirds of this total.

*How citrus fruits are grown:* Citrus trees grow well in tropical and subtropical regions. There are three major areas in the United States where the fruit is grown commercially: the southeast area including Florida and the Gulf States, the western including California and Arizona, and the Rio Grande Valley area of Texas.

Fruit from these areas differs in some aspects. The western area, with its bright sunshine and low humidity, produces brightly colored fruit and juice. The southeastern fruit has somewhat more juice. Fruit produced in the Texas valley has a blend of characteristics of both the western and southeastern fruit.

To produce citrus fruit, trees are usually grown by budding or grafting onto a seedling from a parent tree rather than grown from seeds. Within five or six years these trees will bear a crop.

Citrus trees can have blossoms, immature fruit, and ripe fruit all at the same time. When this occurs, the ripe fruit may be tinged with green color because the tree produces green chlorophyll for the new blooms. This "regreening" does not affect the quality. Once ripened, unlike most fruits, citrus fruit can remain on the tree for weeks or months without becoming overripe or losing quality.

The harvesting, packing, and processing of citrus fruits are highly organized and mechanized. If some ripe fruits show a green color when harvested, they are treated to make their color typical.

Ethylene gas treatment restores the color of fruit grown in the western area. Fruit from the southeastern area gets a coloring bath that brings out the color in the skin. These treatments make the fruit acceptable to consumers but do not affect the flavor or edibility of the fruit pulp or peel.

Juices are extracted mechanically for canning, then blended for optimum quality and flavor, pasteurized, and canned under vacuum. Frozen concentrated juices are made by a moisture-evaporation process which eliminates the water and are then frozen in tubes for packaging.

With improved production and shipping facilities, United States producers meet the rapidly increasing demand for citrus fruit in American markets, plus exporting fruit to many foreign countries.

*Nutritional value:* Citrus fruits are excellent sources of vitamin C. One or two servings of citrus fruit will supply the daily recommended amounts of vitamin C for adults and children.

Depending on the type and variety, citrus fruits also contain varying amounts of vitamin A, the B vitamins, and minerals. Fresh citrus fruits have a low calorie count, usually less than 60, which makes them doubly attractive to dieters.

*How to select:* A selection of top-quality citrus fruits is available throughout the year in the markets. Choose those fruits which are firm, a characteristic color, shiny, and free from blemishes. Heavier fruits contain more juice.

Sizing can be a guideline for the consumer when purchasing citrus fruit. Sizes are assigned according to the number of fruit packed into a standard-size box. For instance, a carton of oranges sized as 56's contains 56 oranges. The larger the number per box, the smaller the fruit. Therefore, lemons sized as 95's are larger than those sized as 115's.

The quality, flavor, and amount of juice in the fruit per box will be the same regardless of the size of the fruit. Selection of which size to buy should be made according to the size that is most plentiful at that time, the size you prefer, and how you plan to use the fruit.

*How to store:* Citrus fruits can be kept in the covered fruit or vegetable section of the refrigerator for several weeks. Wrap the fruit in perforated, clear plastic bags if it is to be stored in another part of the refrigerator. If the peel has been grated, always cover the fruit in foil or clear plastic wrap to keep it from drying out.

Most citrus fruits can be frozen for extended storage. The juice or sections are prepared for freezing by sweetening with sugar and adding ascorbic acid color keeper to preserve the best quality. Use these frozen fruits within 8 to 12 months.

# Types of citrus fruit

Citrus fruits come in an array of bright colors and tart flavors. Each type has its own special characteristics and uses.

*Citron:* This yellow green fruit resembles a lemon. However, citrons are larger than lemons, measuring about six to nine inches in length and have thicker rinds.

Citron is grown for its rind rather than its acid pulp. It is the rind that appears on the market as candied and preserved citron and in packages of mixed candied fruit for use in fruitcakes and cookies.

*Grapefruit:* Grapefruits vary in color from pale yellow to russet to bronze. The tart-sweet pulp may be seedy or seedless. The Marsh, Duncan, and Ruby are the common varieties on the market.

Grapefruit halves, eaten chilled or broiled, can perk you up at breakfast or whet your appetite at dinner. The sections and juices are used as ingredients in recipes. The shaddock, a probable ancestor of grapefruit, often grows as large as a watermelon and weighs 15 to 20 pounds.

*Kumquat:* The smallest member of the citrus family, it has a sweet rind and an acid pulp. Orange in color and oblong to round in shape, kumquats are used in preserves and Oriental dishes.

*Lemon:* Yellow, oval, and very sour lemons are used to enhance many foods. They add flavor and tartness to salads, fish, beverages, sauces, vegetables, and desserts.

Arranged in basket are lemons, limes, and Navel oranges. Around basket (right to left) are tangelos, tangerines, Marsh seedless and Ruby Red grapefruits, and Valencia oranges.

*Lime:* The lime, very acid in flavor, has a green, smooth peel. It is about the same size and shape as the lemon. Limes and lemons are used in the same ways and sometimes may be used interchangeably.

*Limequats* are a tart, pale yellow hybrid developed from lime and kumquat.

*Mandarin:* Small and deep orange, mandarins are round in shape but slightly flattened at the ends. Mandarins are loose-skinned so the rind can be removed easily.

*Tangerines, satsumas,* and *temple oranges* are actually varieties of mandarin. The *calamondin* is a mandarinlike citrus fruit from the Philippines.

*Orange:* The most popular of the citrus fruits has a color ranging from light orange to deep red. Navel and Valencia are the best-known varieties. Navels are seedless and have a small "navel" formation at the blossom end. Valencias are practically seedless and especially juicy.

Oranges are excellent to eat out-of-hand and to use in countless dishes.

*Tangelo:* This hybrid was developed in 1897 by crossing the tangerine and grapefruit. This juicy fruit has a sweet but tart flavor. The rind resembles that of an orange but the flesh is a pale yellow. A tangelo may be used like a tangerine.

*Ugli:* Well named, ugli fruit is an unattractive, puffy fruit—in appearance, but not in flavor. It tastes like orange, grapefruit, and tangerine all in one. Limited numbers are imported from Jamaica.

***Forms available:*** Citrus fruits and citrus fruit products can be purchased in many forms to meet a variety of purposes.

Whole fruit and sections are available fresh, canned, and frozen. These may be packaged separately by types or mixed with other fruits. Juices are also available fresh, canned or bottled, and frozen—as one flavor or a blend of several flavors, concentrated or natural strength.

Other forms of citrus fruit include candied peel, extract, citrus-flavored gelatins and powdered mixes, and liqueurs, such as curacao and Cointreau.

# Uses of citrus fruit

Citrus fruit can be used in any course of a meal and enjoyed at any time of the day. Some appetizers, beverages, salads, entrées, breads, desserts, and snacks are made with one or more citrus fruits as the major ingredient or flavor accent.

As an appetizer, citrus fruits are especially good because their tartness stimulates the appetite without satisfying it.

### Frosted Cocktail

*Pass a tray of hors d'oeuvres with these non-alcoholic cocktails—*

  ½ cup sugar
  ⅔ cup lemon juice
      •    •    •
  ⅔ cup pineapple juice
  2 tablespoons lime juice
  2 unbeaten egg whites
  4 cups finely crushed ice

Cook sugar and ⅔ cup water for 5 minutes; chill. Add lemon juice, pineapple juice, lime juice, egg whites, and crushed ice. Pour *half* the mixture into blender container. Blend till light and frothy, 7 or 8 seconds. Repeat with second half. Serve at once in chilled cocktail glasses with short straws. Serves 8 to 10.

### Spiced Citrus Appetizer Cup

  1 16-ounce can mixed grapefruit
      and orange sections,
      undrained (2 cups)
  3 inches stick cinnamon
      Dash ground cloves
      Dash ground ginger
      Maraschino cherries

Combine all ingredients in saucepan; simmer for 10 minutes. Remove cinnamon stick. Chill. Serve in small glass dishes. Garnish with maraschino cherries. Makes 4 or 5 servings.

Beverages are frequently made using citrus juice as a base or accented with just a dash of juice. Punches and ades owe their refreshing, not-too-sweet flavor to the citrus base. Mixed drinks, such as the daiquiri, Margarita, and screwdriver, are also made with a citrus foundation.

### Citrus Cooler

  ¼ cup frozen orange-grapefruit
      juice concentrate, thawed
  1 pint lemon sherbet
  1 12-ounce bottle ginger ale

Pour thawed concentrate into electric blender container. Add ¾ cup icy cold water and sherbet. Cover; blend 15 seconds. Divide mixture among 4 chilled glasses. Slowly pour in chilled ginger ale to fill each glass. Stir gently; serve *immediately.* Makes 4 servings.

### Tangy Citrus Fizz

  ¾ cup cold orange juice
  1 cup vanilla ice cream
  ½ cup lemon sherbet
  1 teaspoon aromatic bitters
  1 7-ounce bottle lemon-lime
      carbonated beverage

In electric mixer bowl or blender containers, combine juice, ice cream, sherbet, and bitters. Beat or blend till smooth. Pour into 2 tall glasses. Carefully pour in carbonated beverage. Stir gently. Makes 2 servings.

Citrus fruit sections or slices along with crisp lettuce are often used in salads, in molded mixtures, or on fruit platters. Tangy salad dressings also are made with the addition of citrus fruit juice.

## Spiced Mandarin Mold

  1 11-ounce can mandarin orange
      sections
¼ teaspoon salt
  6 inches stick cinnamon
½ teaspoon whole cloves

    • • •

  2 3-ounce packages orange-flavored
      gelatin
  3 tablespoons lemon juice
½ cup broken walnuts

Drain mandarins; reserving syrup. Add water to syrup to make 1¾ cups. In saucepan, combine syrup mixture, salt, cinnamon, and cloves. Cover and simmer 10 minutes; remove from heat. Let stand covered 10 minutes. Strain.

Add gelatin to syrup mixture; stir over low heat till gelatin is dissolved. Add 2 cups cold water and lemon juice. Chill till partially set. Stir in mandarins and nuts; turn into a 6½-cup mold. Chill till firm. Serves 6 to 8.

## Low-Cal Fruit Bowl

  1 medium grapefruit, chilled
  2 medium oranges, chilled
  1 ripe medium banana
  1 cup chilled sliced fresh
      strawberries
½ cup chilled honeydew balls
    Lettuce
    Mint sprigs
    Low-Cal Snow Dressing

Peel and section grapefruit and oranges, reserving juices. Peel and slice banana; brush with reserved fruit juices. Combine grapefruit and orange sections, banana, strawberries, and honeydew balls in lettuce-lined bowl. Garnish with mint. Serve salad with Low-Cal Snow Dressing. Makes 4 servings.

*Low-Cal Snow Dressing:* Combine 1 cup plain yogurt, 4 teaspoons sugar, 1 teaspoon lemon juice, and dash salt. Chill thoroughly.

## Heavenly Orange Fluff

  2 3-ounce packages orange-
      flavored gelatin
  1 13½-ounce can crushed pineapple
  1 6-ounce can frozen orange juice
      concentrate, thawed
  2 11-ounce cans mandarin oranges,
      drained
  1 3¾-ounce package *instant*
      lemon pudding mix
  1 cup cold milk
  1 cup whipping cream

Dissolve gelatin in 2½ cups boiling water; add undrained pineapple and concentrate. Chill till partially set. Fold in mandarins; pour into 13x9x2-inch pan. Chill till firm. Beat pudding and milk with rotary beater till smooth. Whip cream and fold into pudding. Spread over gelatin; chill. Makes 12 to 15 servings.

To section citrus fruit: first peel and remove excess membrane. Then cut into center between one section and membrane. Slide knife down other side of section next to membrane.

## Orange-Apricot Ring

    2 16-ounce cans apricot halves
    2 3-ounce packages orange-flavored
        gelatin
    1 6-ounce can frozen orange juice
        concentrate
    2 tablespoons lemon juice
    1 7-ounce bottle (about 1 cup)
        lemon-lime carbonated
        beverage, chilled

Drain apricots, reserving 1½ cups syrup. Purée apricots in sieve or blender. Heat reserved apricot syrup to boiling; dissolve orange-flavored gelatin and dash salt in syrup. Add purée, juice concentrate, and lemon juice; stir till concentrate is melted. Slowly pour chilled carbonated beverage down side of pan; mix gently. Pour gelatin mixture into 6½-cup ring mold. Chill till firm. Makes 10 to 12 servings.

## Summer Fruit Platter

*Add this salad to the buffet menu—*

    Whole fresh pineapple
    Apples
    Fresh pears
    Fresh strawberries, sliced
        • • •
    Oranges, sliced crosswise
    Cantaloupe wedges
    Stewed prunes, drained
    Lime Honey *or* Marshmallow
        Blizzard

Chill fruit. Halve pineapple lengthwise; remove hard core. Scoop out fruit and cut into chunks. Cube apples and pears; toss with pineapple chunks and sliced strawberries. Pile fruit mixture into pineapple shells. Arrange on a tray with orange slices, cantaloupe wedges, and prunes. If desired, garnish with sprigs of mint. Serve Lime Honey *or* Marshmallow Blizzard Dressing with the fruit platter.

*Lime Honey:* Blend together ¼ cup honey with 2 tablespoons lime juice. Add dash salt.

*Marshmallow Blizzard:* To half of 7-ounce jar marshmallow creme, add 1 tablespoon *each* orange juice and lemon juice. With electric or rotary beater, beat till very fluffy. Fold in ¼ cup mayonnaise or salad dressing.

## Fluffy Citrus Dressing

    1 egg
    ½ cup sugar
    1 tablespoon grated orange peel
    2 teaspoons grated lemon peel
    2 tablespoons lemon juice
    1 cup whipping cream

In saucepan beat egg; add sugar, peel, and lemon juice. Cook and stir over *low* heat till thick, 5 minutes. Cool well. Whip cream and fold into egg mixture. Chill. Makes 2⅓ cups.

Citrus fruits make attractive garnishes or accompaniments with entrées, as well as adding flavor to the meat dishes, to sauces for meat, and to stuffings.

## Orange Pot Roast

    1½ teaspoons salt
    ½ teaspoon ground cumin
    ¼ teaspoon ground cloves
    ⅛ teaspoon pepper
    1 3- or 4-pound chuck pot roast
    1 tablespoon shortening
    1 6-ounce can frozen orange juice
        concentrate, thawed
        • • •
    1 cup bias-cut celery slices
    1 5-ounce can bamboo shoots,
        drained
    1 11-ounce can mandarin oranges,
        drained
    1 tablespoon cornstarch

Combine salt, cumin, cloves, and pepper. Make small slits in chuck roast; in each slit insert some of the spice mixture. Melt shortening in large skillet or Dutch oven. Brown meat on both sides. Add concentrate and ¾ cup water. Cover and simmer till tender, 2½ to 3 hours.

Add celery; simmer, covered, 10 to 12 minutes. Arrange bamboo shoots and mandarin oranges on top of roast. Cook, covered, 5 to 7 minutes. Remove meat to warm platter.

Skim fat from liquid. Blend cornstarch and 2 tablespoons cold water; slowly add to liquid in pan, stirring constantly. Cook and stir till thick. Serve gravy with meat and pass vegetables in serving bowl. Makes 6 to 8 servings.

## Mediterranean Sauce

¼ cup brown sugar
1 tablespoon cornstarch
⅛ teaspoon salt
⅛ teaspoon ground cloves
1 cup orange juice
2 tablespoons lemon juice
½ cup chopped dried figs

In saucepan combine brown sugar and corn-starch. Blend in salt, cloves, orange juice, and lemon juice. Bring to boil, stirring constantly. Add figs; cover and simmer 5 minutes. Serve sauce hot with pork. Makes 1½ cups sauce.

Vegetable flavors are often sparked by zesty citrus juice. The juice can be added to vegetables or to the sauces for the vegetable. Citrus peel or segments also add a colorful appearance and distinctive taste.

## Ambrosia Potato Bake

½ lemon, thinly sliced
½ orange, thinly sliced
6 to 7 cups sliced, cooked *or*
    canned sweet potatoes, drained

      •   •   •

1 8¾-ounce can crushed
    pineapple
½ cup brown sugar
½ cup butter, melted
½ teaspoon salt

      •   •   •

½ cup shredded coconut
  Maraschino cherries

Alternate lemon, orange, and sweet potato slices in an 11½x7½x1½-inch baking dish. Combine crushed pineapple, brown sugar, butter, and salt; pour over potatoes and fruit. Sprinkle coconut over top; garnish with cherries. Bake at 350° for 30 minutes. Serves 8 to 10.

### *A showcase dessert*

Delicately flavored with orange and lemon, Citrus Chiffon Pie is a treasured recipe to make for those extra special occasions.

Breads can be flavored with citrus peel or juice in the dough, filling, or glaze. A hint of citrus in the fragrance of freshly baked bread gives it a tantalizing aroma.

## Citrus Coffee Cake

    2 tablespoons butter or margarine
    1 tablespoon frozen orange juice
       concentrate, thawed
    1 teaspoon lemon juice
    1/3 cup sugar
    1/4 teaspoon ground cinnamon
    1/4 cup coarsely chopped pecans
    1 8-ounce package refrigerated
       buttermilk biscuits

Melt butter in 8x1 1/2-inch round cake pan. Stir in orange juice concentrate, lemon juice, sugar, cinnamon, and chopped pecans. Top with biscuits. Bake at 350° for 25 minutes. Cool 1 minute; invert on serving plate. Serve warm.

## Orange Coffee Braid

    2 packages active dry yeast
    5 to 5 1/2 cups sifted all-purpose
       flour
    1 1/4 cups milk
       . . .
    1/2 cup sugar
    1/3 cup frozen orange juice
       concentrate, thawed
    6 tablespoons butter or margarine
    1 teaspoon shredded lemon peel
    1/2 teaspoon salt
    1 egg
       . . .
    3/4 cup sifted confectioners' sugar
    1 tablespoon frozen orange juice
       concentrate, thawed
       Toasted slivered almonds

In large mixer bowl, combine yeast and 2 2/3 *cups* flour. Heat milk, sugar, 1/3 cup juice, butter, peel, and salt just till warm, stirring occasionally to melt butter. Add to dry mixture in mixing bowl; add egg. Beat at low speed with electric mixer for 1/2 minute, scraping sides of bowl constantly. Beat 3 minutes at high speed. By hand, stir in enough of remaining all-purpose flour to make a soft dough.

Turn out on lightly floured surface and knead till smooth, about 8 to 10 minutes. Place in greased bowl, turning once to grease surface. Cover and let rise in a warm place till doubled, about 1 1/2 hours. Punch down; divide dough in half and let rest about 10 minutes.

From one-half of dough, cut off one-third and set aside. Divide remaining two-thirds into three equal portions. Roll each portion into a 12-inch strand. Place the three strands on greased baking sheet and braid.

Divide reserved one-third of dough into three equal portions and roll each portion into 12-inch strand. Braid and place atop first braid. Repeat with second half of dough, forming two braids as before. Cover; let rise till almost doubled, about 45 minutes. Bake at 350° for 30 to 35 minutes.

Beat together the confectioners' sugar, 1 tablespoon thawed orange juice concentrate, and 1 tablespoon water. Brush over tops of braids when they come from the oven. Sprinkle tops with almonds. Makes 2 braids.

Desserts made with citrus fruit are colorful and flavorful. The citrus flavor can be incorporated into cake, pastry, pie, pudding, sauce, and ice cream. Citrus segments, twists, cartwheels, curls, and shredded peel are attractive as garnishes on desserts. (See *Fruit* and individual citrus fruits for additional information.)

## Orange Velvet

    1 3-ounce package orange-
       flavored gelatin
    1/2 cup sugar
    1 cup water
    1 cup light corn syrup
    1 cup orange juice
    2 tablespoons lemon juice
    2 cups milk
    2 cups light cream

In saucepan combine gelatin and sugar; stir in water and corn syrup. Bring to boiling, stirring till gelatin dissolves. Remove from heat. Stir in juices; cool. Add milk, cream, and a dash salt. Freeze in ice cream freezer according to freezer directions. Garnish servings with orange slices, as desired. Makes 2 quarts.

## Citrus Cobbler

    1 16-ounce can grapefruit sections
    1 11-ounce can mandarin orange
        sections
    ½ cup brown sugar
    3 tablespoons all-purpose flour
    7 tablespoons butter or margarine
    1 cup sifted all-purpose flour
    1 tablespoon granulated sugar
    1½ teaspoons baking powder
    1 slightly beaten egg

Combine *undrained* fruits; divide among 6 individual bakers or place in 8x8x2-inch baking dish. Mix brown sugar with the 3 tablespoons flour; sprinkle over fruit. Dot with *3 tablespoons* butter or margarine. Heat at 425° for 15 minutes. Sift together 1 cup flour, granulated sugar, baking powder, and ¼ teaspoon salt; cut in the remaining butter. Add enough milk to egg to make ½ cup; stir into dry ingredients. Drop mixture by spoonfuls on hot fruit to form biscuits. Sprinkle with a little sugar and cinnamon. Bake at 425° for 20 to 25 minutes or till biscuits are lightly browned. Serve warm with cream, if desired. Makes 6 servings.

## Mandarin Soufflé

    ¼ cup sugar
    1 envelope unflavored gelatin
    4 well-beaten egg yolks
    ¾ cup tangerine *or* orange juice
    2 tablespoons lemon juice
    2 tablespoons grated orange peel
    4 egg whites
    2 tablespoons sugar
    1 cup whipping cream

In a saucepan combine the ¼ cup sugar and gelatin; blend in egg yolks, then tangerine or orange juice, and lemon juice. Cook and stir over low heat till gelatin dissolves and mixture thickens slightly. Stir in orange peel; cool mixture to room temperature.

Beat egg whites to soft peaks; gradually add 2 tablespoons sugar, beating to stiff peaks. Whip cream. Fold gelatin into egg whites, then fold in whipped cream. Turn into a 5-cup melon mold. Chill overnight or till set. Unmold on platter. Garnish with whipped cream and mandarin oranges, if desired. Serves 6 to 8.

## Tangelo Chiffon Pie

    1 envelope unflavored gelatin
    ½ cup sugar
    4 eggs, separated
    ½ cup lemon juice
    ¾ cup tangelo *or* tangerine juice
    ½ teaspoon grated lemon peel
    ½ teaspoon grated tangelo *or*
        tangerine peel
    ⅓ cup sugar
    1 9-inch *baked* pastry shell*

In a saucepan mix gelatin, ½ cup sugar, and dash salt. Beat together egg yolks and fruit juices; stir into gelatin. Cook and stir over medium heat till mixture comes to boiling. Remove from heat; mix in peels. Chill, stirring occasionally, till partially set. Beat egg whites till soft peaks form. Gradually add ⅓ cup sugar; beat to stiff peaks. Fold in gelatin. Pile into pastry shell; chill till firm. Garnish with dollops of whipped cream and tangelo *or* tangerine sections, if desired.

## Citrus Chiffon Pie

    1 envelope unflavored gelatin
    ½ cup sugar
    4 egg yolks
    ½ cup orange juice
    ⅓ cup lemon juice
    ½ teaspoon grated orange peel
    ½ teaspoon grated lemon peel
    4 egg whites
    ⅓ cup sugar
    1 9-inch *baked* pastry shell*

In saucepan thoroughly mix gelatin, the ½ cup sugar, and dash salt. Beat together egg yolks, juices, and ¼ cup water; stir into gelatin. Cook and stir over medium heat just till mixture comes to boiling and gelatin is completely dissolved. Remove from heat; stir in orange and lemon peel. Chill, stirring occasionally, till mixture is partially set.

Beat egg whites till soft peaks form. Gradually add the ⅓ cup sugar, beating till stiff peaks form; fold in gelatin mixture. Pile into cooled baked pastry shell. Chill till firm. Garnish with whipped cream and a sprinkle of shredded orange peel, if desired.

*(See *Pastry* for recipe.)

**CITY CHICKEN**—Boneless cubes of veal threaded together on a skewer and then cooked. The skewered cubes are coated with crumbs, browned, and then baked in a small amount of liquid. (See also *Veal*.)

## City Chicken

      2 pounds veal, cut in 1½-inch
         cubes
      ⅔ cup fine saltine cracker crumbs
      1½ teaspoons salt
      1 teaspoon paprika
      ¾ teaspoon poultry seasoning
      1 slightly beaten egg
      2 tablespoons milk
      3 tablespoons shortening
      1 chicken bouillon cube

Thread veal cubes onto 6 short skewers. Combine crumbs, salt, paprika, and poultry seasoning. Combine egg and milk. Dip meat in egg mixture, then in crumbs. Brown slowly on all sides in hot shortening. Dissolve bouillon cube in ½ cup boiling water; add to meat. Cover; bake at 350° for 45 minutes. Uncover; bake 30 minutes more. Makes 6 servings.

**CIVET** (*siv′ it*)—A French stew made with rabbit or other furred game, wine, onion, mushrooms, and seasonings. The blood of the animal is used to thicken the stew.

**CLABBER**—Unpasteurized milk that has soured naturally and formed a thickened mass in which there is no separation of curd from whey. Sometimes called bonny-clabber, it is popular in some countries served chilled as a beverage. When thickly clotted, it is eaten as a dessert; sugar and flavoring may be added. (See also *Milk*.)

**CLAM**—A shellfish in which the edible flesh is encased in two shells joined together at the back. Prized for their distinctive flavor, clams are a part of many traditions. Undoubtedly, the most elaborate and ceremonial is the "clambake." First staged by the Indians, it involves cooking clams, fish, and corn on heated stones in a shallow pit. Covered with wet rockweed, the food is cooked by steam. Today's clambakes often include additional foods such as lobster and chicken, but the cooking method is the same. For an inland clambake, substitute a barbecue grill for the open pit and a wet canvas for the wet rockweed.

## Individual Clambake

      48 soft-shelled clams, in shells
      8 live whole lobsters
      4 2- to 2½-pound ready-to-cook
         broiler-fryer chickens, halved
      ½ cup butter or margarine, melted
      8 whole ears of corn
         Rockweed
      1 pound butter, melted

Thoroughly wash clams in shells. Cover with salt water (⅓ cup salt to 1 gallon water); let stand 15 minutes. Rinse; repeat twice. Rinse off lobsters with salt water. For chickens, break joints of drumstick, hip, and wing so birds will stay flat. Brush chickens with ½ cup melted butter or margarine; broil over *hot* coals, skin side down for about 5 minutes.

Turn back husks of corn and strip off silk with a stiff brush. Lay husks back in position.

Tear off 3-foot lengths of 18-inch wide heavy foil. Place 1 sheet crosswise over another sheet. Repeat making total of 8 individual packages. Lay a handful of rockweed in center of each. Cut eight 18-inch squares cheesecloth; place 1 square atop rockweed in each package.

For each package arrange the following: 6 live clams in shells, 1 live lobster, 1 precooked chicken half, and 1 ear of corn. Securely tie cheesecloth around meat and vegetable, opposite ends together. Seal the foil, opposite ends together, using the drugstore wrap. Place on grill, seam side up, over *hot* coals and cook for 45 minutes. To test for doneness, the chicken drumstick should move up and down easily in socket. When the chicken is done, the clambake is ready. Serve with individual cups of hot melted butter. Makes 8 servings.

### *Modern clambake*

Rockweed adds authenticity to Individual → Clambake cooked on a grill. Watermelon and cold beer complete the outdoor feast.

***How clams are harvested:*** Clam digging is not only an amateur's delight but also a commercial business. Clamming on a small scale involves digging with your hands or a rake-type instrument for the **soft clams** found in the tidal flats. Commercially, fishermen employ long-handled rakes, tongs, or dredges for digging hard clams living at much greater depth.

***Nutritional value:*** Clams provide protein and minerals including phosphorus, calcium, and iron. Relatively low in calories, four large soft-shell clams or five hard clams contain about 80 calories.

***Types of clams:*** Several varieties of clams are marketed, each supplied from a different coastal region. The hard clam (round clam), the soft-shell clam (longneck clam), and the surf clam are found along the Atlantic coast. The hard clam is given the Indian name *quahog* in the New England area where the term clam is used only for the soft-shell variety. In the Middle Atlantic states and southward, clam refers to the hard clam.

The soft-shell clam, found in the tidal flats, appears chiefly in the Chesapeake Bay although some are found farther north. The hard clam, often living more than 50 feet deep, is found south of Cape Cod down to Texas. Surf clams live along the Middle Atlantic coastline.

The small-sized hard clams are divided into littlenecks and cherrystones and are served raw on the half shell. The larger hard clams, called chowder clams, are used for chowders and soups. Soft-shell clams are also divided into classes: the larger sizes are known as in-shells, and the smaller sizes are called steamers.

The Pacific coast varieties of clams include Pismo, razor, geoduck, Washington or butter, heart cockle, and rock cockle (rock clam or common littleneck). Each varies in flavor and use but should not be confused with the Atlantic varieties.

***How to select:*** Clams are available in the shell, shucked, or canned. When purchasing hard clams, gently tap each shell. It should close tightly to indicate the clam is alive. A gaping shell that does not close means that the clam is dead and should not be used. With other varieties, a constriction of the siphon (tube through which clam takes in food and oxygen and eliminates wastes) is noticeable when touched. Clams in the shell are sold by the dozen or by the pound.

If the clam muscle has been removed from the shell, the clams are sold as shucked clams. Packaged in various-sized containers, they should appear plump with clear liquor and be free of shell particles. Shucked clams are also available frozen.

Many varieties of clams are preserved by canning and are marketed either whole or minced. Other clam products available include chowder, juice, broth, and nectar.

***How to store:*** Shell clams will remain alive and fresh for several days if refrigerated immediately after being dug or purchased. Shucked clams, too, require refrigeration and may be stored for several days when properly handled. Frozen clams should not be thawed until ready to use and after thawing, they should not be refrozen.

***How to prepare:*** Wash clams thoroughly to remove all surface sand. Allow clams to stand in cold salt water (1/3 cup salt to 1 gallon water) for 15 minutes. Rinse and repeat two more times. This permits clams to open and discharge sand which then settles to the bottom of container.

Clams may be shucked either before or after cooking, depending upon how they are served. To open clams, insert knife between shell halves and pry apart (see page 564). If steamed before shucking, the shell will open during steaming. The shells of soft clams and surf clams are not as tight-fitting and so are easier to open.

***How to use:*** Clams served on the half shell make an elegant appetizer. Discard the top shell, cut the muscle free but leave it in the bottom half shell. Other clam appetizers include dips and canapés.

The popular clam chowder, with its many regional variations, is often considered a specialty. Clams are also used in seafood salads, casseroles, soufflés, or other main dishes. Fried clams are also favorites. (See also *Shellfish*.)

## Clam Puff

- 2 7½-ounce cans minced clams
  Milk
- 1 cup fine saltine cracker crumbs (24 crackers)
- 2 tablespoons instant minced onion
- 4 well-beaten eggs
- 2 tablespoons snipped parsley
- ½ teaspoon salt
  Dash bottled hot pepper sauce

Drain clams, reserving liquor; add milk to liquor to make 1 cup. Combine milk mixture with crumbs and minced onion. Let stand 15 minutes. Fold in clams, eggs, parsley, salt, and bottled hot pepper sauce. Pour into *ungreased* 1½-quart soufflé dish. Bake at 325° till knife inserted off center comes out clean, about 60 to 65 minutes. Makes 6 servings.

## Clam Cocktail Dunk

- 2 3-ounce packages cream cheese, softened
- 2 teaspoons lemon juice
- 3 drops onion juice
- 1 teaspoon Worcestershire sauce
- ¼ teaspoon salt
- 3 drops bottled hot pepper sauce
- 1 7½-ounce can minced clams, chilled and drained
- 1 tablespoon snipped parsley

In small mixing bowl combine softened cream cheese, lemon juice, onion juice, Worcestershire sauce, salt, and bottled hot pepper sauce. With electric or rotary beater, beat till light and fluffy. Stir in drained clams and snipped parsley. Serve clam dunk with assorted crackers or crisp relishes. Makes 1¼ cups.

A delicacy for dining—Steamed Clams served in a big mesh steamer. Accompany with clam broth, melted butter, and lemon wedges. For ease-of-eating, provide guests with bibs.

To open hard-shell clam, hold shell in palm of hand with hinge against palm. Insert slender knife between shell halves.

Carefully cut around clam between shell halves, twisting knife slightly to pry open shell. Lift up top shell-half with thumb.

Cut clam muscle free from each shell half. To serve clam on the half shell, remove one-half of shell before serving.

## Steamed Clams

> 2 dozen soft-shell clams in shells
>   (steamers)
> Salt
>       . . .
> Butter or margarine, melted
> Lemon wedges

Thoroughly wash clams. Cover with salt water, using ⅓ cup salt to 1 gallon cold water. Let stand 15 minutes; rinse thoroughly. Repeat soaking in salt water two more times.

Place clams in shells on rack in kettle. Add 1 cup hot water; cover tightly and steam just till shells open, about 5 minutes. Drain off broth and reserve. Serve in shell or cut out and serve on the half shell (see directions at left). Serve clams with reserved clam broth, melted butter, and lemon wedges. Makes 4 servings.

## Clam-Mushroom Bake

> 1 dozen large hard-shell clams
>   (½ cup clam meat) *or* 1
>   7½-ounce can minced clams,
>   drained
> 1 3-ounce can chopped mushrooms,
>   drained
> ¼ cup chopped onion
> 3 tablespoons butter or margarine
>       . . .
> 2 tablespoons all-purpose flour
> Dash salt
> Dash pepper
> ½ cup milk
>       . . .
> ½ cup soft bread crumbs
> 2 tablespoons butter or margarine,
>   melted

For fresh clams, prepare Steamed Clams (see above) *or* open unsteamed clams (see directions at left). Remove edible portion; chop.

Cook mushrooms and onion in 3 tablespoons butter till tender but not brown. Blend in flour, salt, and pepper. Add milk all at once. Cook quickly, stirring constantly, till mixture is thickened and bubbly. Stir in clams. Pour into 4 baking shells. Combine bread crumbs and melted butter; sprinkle atop each shell. Bake at 400° till lightly browned, about 10 to 15 minutes. Makes 4 servings.

**CLAM CHOWDER**—A thickened soup made with clams and usually containing salt pork or bacon, potatoes, and/or other vegetables. Popular where its ingredients are readily available, clam chowder is the subject of a continuous controversy about its "true" character. Although many variations exist, most of the debate concerns the liquid used. New England-style clam chowder is made with milk; Manhattan-style clam chowder uses water and tomatoes or tomato juice. (See also *Chowder.*)

## Hogate's Clam Chowder

2 dozen medium hard-shell clams
2 ounces salt pork (¾ cup), diced
2 cups diced, peeled potatoes
    (about 3 medium)
1 cup chopped onion
1 teaspoon dried thyme leaves,
    crushed
1 16-ounce can tomatoes
2 tablespoons all-purpose flour

Thoroughly wash clams. Cover with salt water (⅓ cup salt to 1 gallon cold water). Let stand 15 minutes. Rinse; repeat 2 more times. Place clams on rack in kettle; add 6 cups hot water. Cover tightly; steam just till shells open, 5 to 10 minutes. Remove clams reserving 4 cups cooking liquor. Shuck clams and dice.

Brown salt pork in large saucepan. Add *2 cups* of the reserved liquor, potatoes, onion, and thyme. Cook till potatoes are almost tender, about 20 minutes. Add tomatoes and remaining 2 cups reserved liquor. Bring to boiling.

Blend all-purpose flour with ¼ cup cold water. Stir into chowder; cook, stirring constantly, till thickened and bubbly. Add diced clams; heat through. Makes 8 servings.

**CLARET** (*klar' it*)—A light, red table wine. All red wines from Bordeaux are commonly termed claret by the British and Americans. However, the clarets of today are not the same as those wines which were originally labeled claret. During the early history of wine making, red wines were fermented only briefly, sometimes for only two weeks—the time it took to ship the wine from France to England.

Many of the classic Bordeaux wines are named after the wine estate or château where they are produced. The first growth of finest wines are Château Margaux, Château Lafite, Château Latour, and Château Haut-Brion. Other less expensive but good clarets are labeled for the Bordeaux district from which they come: Médoc, St. Émilion, Graves, and Pomerol.

The production of fine clarets, however, is not limited to European vineyards. California claret is one of the most popular, domestic red wines on the market. Made from the Cabernet Sauvignon grape, it is labeled Cabernet or Cabernet Sauvignon.

Although personal preference determines the selection and use of red dinner wines, claret is generally served with meat. Used as an ingredient in cooking, it adds a distinctive flavor to many well-known meat dishes. It is a favorite used in preparing the rich sauces which are often served with game, such as pheasant and quail. (See also *Wines and Spirits.*)

## Beef Claret Barbecue

½ cup salad oil
½ cup claret
2 tablespoons finely snipped
    candied ginger
2 tablespoons catsup
2 tablespoons molasses
½ teaspoon salt
½ teaspoon curry powder
½ teaspoon pepper
1 large clove garlic, minced
    • • •
1 pound sirloin steak, cut in
    1-inch cubes
    • • •
1 green pepper, cut in
    1-inch squares

In glass bowl or shallow dish, combine all ingredients except meat and green pepper. Add beef cubes; let stand at room temperature for 1 hour, or refrigerate overnight. Remove beef cubes, reserving marinade. Arrange on skewers with green pepper squares. Cook over *medium-hot* coals for 12 to 15 minutes, brushing several times with marinade. (Use rotating skewer or turn once during cooking.) Serves 3 or 4.

**CLARIFIED BUTTER**—Clear, oil-like butter poured from melted butter leaving water and salt behind. As butter melts over low heat or hot water, without stirring, the fat rises and the brine sinks to the bottom. When cooled, the oil-like top layer can be carefully poured off.

Clarified butter is called for in a number of French sauce recipes because it can be heated to high temperatures without burning or browning. It is also particularly suitable for quickly sautéing delicately flavored foods. (See also *Butter.*)

**CLARIFY**—To make a liquid or fat clear by separating solid particles from the liquid. One example is the melting of butter to clarify it. To clarify hydrogenated fat that has been used for deep-fat frying, pour an equal amount of hot water over the fat; heat for 10 minutes. Strain through a cloth. Chill until the layer of clarified fat is hard, then drain off the water.

**CLARY**—An herb, one of the strong-scented mints, whose leaves and flowers are used for flavoring foods and beverages. Clary, which tastes like a mixture of mint and sage, is easily grown in herb gardens. It was formerly used like sage in cooking, but now its main use is as one of the herbs used to flavor vermouth. (See also *Herb.*)

**CLEAVER**—A heavy, hatchetlike, wide-bladed utensil with a squared, blunt end. A meat cleaver is used to chop through bony tissue in meats or poultry, and its broad side is used to flatten certain meat cuts as when butterflying chops or tenderloin slices. (See also *Utensil.*)

**CLOTTED CREAM**—Very thick, rich cream that has coagulated after being scalded. (See also *Devonshire Cream.*)

**CLOVE** *(segment)*—A segment of a large plant bulb, such as garlic.

**CLOVE** *(spice)*—Nail-shaped, reddish brown, dried bud used as a spice. This fragrant spice grows on a 30- to 40-foot tropical evergreen tree. The name clove comes from the word for nail, *clou* in French or *clavus* in Latin.

Little is known about the history of cloves, but records of the third century B.C. in China report the use of cloves as a breath sweetener, as when courtiers were ordered to hold cloves in their mouths when addressing the emperor.

Large clove forests were first discovered on the Molucca or Spice Islands in the Indian Ocean. Early explorers were impressed by the beauty of the clove tree and the spicy fragrance wafting from the trees. These explorers noted that natives of these islands planted a clove tree at the birth of each child and prized them as a record of ages: a tribe's strength could be noted by the number of trees it had.

During the Middle Ages, all spices reaching Europe had to be carried overland, for the most part, by way of Egypt. This slow means of import made cloves an extremely expensive item—a pound (4,000 to 7,000 cloves) of this spice cost $20.

Between the fourteenth and seventeenth centuries, the major European powers raced each other to find the closest sea routes to the Spice Islands. The establishment of these water routes led to wars between Europeans and native islanders to secure rights to the clove business. Although the islanders fought fiercely, they were greatly outnumbered and soon lost the spice trade to the Europeans.

During the seventeenth century, the Dutch gained control of the Spice Islands and thus controlled the majority of clove trees. To ensure complete control, the Dutch destroyed all clove trees growing on other islands, confining production to their own territory. In 1760, when spice prices failed to satisfy the Dutch, they attempted to raise prices by burning large numbers of cloves and nutmegs at Amsterdam.

The Dutch spice monopoly was maintained for over a century. It was broken in 1770 when the Governor of Mauritius, an island near Madagascar, stole clove seeds and started growing them on his island.

Ironically, although the finest cloves are still found on the Spice Islands, these are not exported but are used by the Indonesians to scent tobacco. Today, the world's supply of this spice comes mainly from the islands of Madagascar and Zanzibar, off the east coast of Africa.

The unopened clove buds must be hand picked at exactly the right stage of maturity to be useful as a spice. Harvest season lasts from October to February.

After being picked, the cloves are spread on mats where they are dried by exposure to the sun and smoke from wood fires. During this six to eight day period, cloves turn from red to a deep brown color and lose at least half of their original weight.

Cloves imported into the United States arrive in whole form. Grinding companies thoroughly clean all the cloves and then grind a portion of them. Both whole and ground cloves are available on the grocery store spice shelf.

The strong, pungent-sweet flavor of cloves seems to "belong" to ham. A small piece of clove flavor perks up condiments, fruit butters, relishes, pickled fruits, spiced cakes and cookies, mincemeat, chocolate dishes, pork roast, stewed fruits, and apple pie. An onion studded with a few cloves adds a subtle spicy flavor to stew. A little of this strong, aromatic spice adds a lot of flavor, so remember to use cloves sparingly. (See also *Spice*.)

## Refrigerator Crisps

    1 cup shortening
    ½ cup granulated sugar
    ½ cup brown sugar
    1 egg
    2 tablespoons milk
    2¼ cups sifted all-purpose flour
    ½ teaspoon baking soda
    ½ teaspoon salt
    1 teaspoon ground cinnamon
    ¼ teaspoon ground nutmeg
    ¼ teaspoon ground cloves
    ½ cup finely chopped walnuts

Cream together shortening and sugar. Add egg and milk; beat well. Sift together flour, baking soda, salt, cinnamon, nutmeg, and cloves; stir into creamed mixture. Stir in finely chopped walnuts. Shape in rolls 2½ inches in diameter. Wrap in waxed paper; chill well.

Slice about ¼ inch thick. Place 1 inch apart on lightly greased cookie sheet. Bake at 375° till delicately browned, about 5 to 7 minutes. Remove at once to rack. Makes 6 dozen.

## Spicy Apricot Mold

    1 16-ounce can apricot halves
    1 8¾-ounce can pineapple tidbits
    2 tablespoons vinegar
    1 teaspoon whole cloves
    4 inches stick cinnamon
        • • •
    2 3-ounce packages orange-
        flavored gelatin
    ¾ cup boiling water
    ¾ cup apricot nectar
    ½ cup dairy sour cream

Drain the apricot halves and pineapple tidbits, reserving syrups. Combine syrups with vinegar, whole cloves, and stick cinnamon; bring to boil. Simmer 10 minutes; strain. Add hot water to make 2 cups. Pour over *one* package orange-flavored gelatin; stir to dissolve gelatin. Chill till mixture is partially set.

Fold in *well-drained* apricot halves, halved, and pineapple. Pour into 6½-cup ring mold. Chill till mixture is *almost* firm.

Meanwhile, dissolve remaining package orange-flavored gelatin in boiling water; stir in apricot nectar. Chill till mixture is partially set; whip till fluffy. Swirl in dairy sour cream. Pour sour cream mixture over first layer. Chill till firm, at least 8 hours. Makes 8 servings.

## Pickled Onion Rings

*Pile these on hamburgers for a special flavor —*

    1 cup water
    1 cup white vinegar
    ¼ cup sugar
    ½ teaspoon salt
    6 inches stick cinnamon,
        broken in pieces
    2 teaspoons whole cloves
   10 drops red food coloring
    1 large sweet onion, thinly
        sliced and separated in
        rings (about 4 cups)

In small saucepan combine water, white vinegar, sugar, salt, stick cinnamon, and whole cloves. Simmer, covered, 10 minutes; strain. Add food coloring; pour hot mixture over onion rings. Chill at least 4 hours, turning occasionally. Drain thoroughly before serving.

Club cheese—
A soft, spreadable
cheese blend.

**CLUB CHEESE**—A cheese product made by blending one or more aged, sharp, natural cheeses. Although club cheeses originated in Canada, they are extensively produced in the United States today. Natural cheeses are ground and mixed without heating or pasteurizing and then packed cold—thus, the name cold-pack often given to club cheese. Condiments, wine, or flavorings such as smoke are often added to the cheese. The resulting club cheese is soft, spreadable, and keeps well when stored in the refrigerator.

Usually packaged in jars, rolls, or links, club cheeses make flavorful additions to appetizers, snacks, sandwiches, and desserts. (See also *Cheese*.)

## Cheese-Stuffed Mushrooms

2 6-ounce cans broiled mushroom
    crowns*, drained (2 cups)
1 tablespoon finely chopped onion
1 teaspoon salad oil

· · ·

¼ cup finely chopped salami
¼ cup smoke-flavored cheese
    spread (club cheese)
1 tablespoon catsup
    Fine soft bread crumbs

Hollow out mushroom crowns and chop enough pieces to make 3 tablespoons; in skillet cook mushroom pieces and onion in oil. Stir in salami, cheese spread, and catsup. Stuff into mushroom crowns; sprinkle with crumbs. Bake on baking sheet at 425° till hot, about 6 to 8 minutes.

*Or use 2 pints fresh mushrooms. Wash; trim off tips of stems. Remove stems and chop enough to make ⅓ cup. Continue as above.

**CLUB SANDWICH**—A hearty triple-decker sandwich made with three toast slices. The filling layers consist of various meats—usually chicken, turkey, bacon, or ham—lettuce, and tomato. (See also *Sandwich*.)

## Club Sandwich

3 slices toasted sandwich bread
    Butter or margarine

· · ·

    Lettuce
    Sliced cooked chicken *or*
        turkey
    Mayonnaise or salad dressing
2 or 3 thin slices tomato
2 or 3 slices cooked bacon

Spread toast with butter. Top first slice with lettuce and chicken *or* turkey. Spread with mayonnaise or salad dressing. Top with second toast slice. Add tomato and bacon. Top with third toast slice. Anchor with 4 wooden picks. Cut diagonally in quarters. Makes 1 serving.

**CLUB STEAK**—The first steak cut from the center loin section of beef, usually identified by a rib bone along its side. The large muscle is the loin eye. (See *Beef, Steak* for additional information.)

**COAGULATE**—To change the form of a food from a liquid or semiliquid to a solid or semisolid substance. Examples of coagulation include the formation of a tender milk curd when rennet is added to slightly warm milk, or the solidification of semiliquid egg white and semisolid egg yolk when egg is heated.

**COAT**—To cover one food with a layer of another, such as flour, bread crumbs, or sugar, in order to add texture to the food or to protect its inner moistness.

Coating may involve one of two techniques. A food may itself be moist enough to coat with a fine substance as when cookies hot from the oven are rolled in sugar. When the outer surface of a food is dry, or a thicker coating is desired, the food is first dipped in a liquid, often water, beaten egg, butter, or milk, then in the coating.

The quick and neat method to coat chicken —shake the chicken pieces with the dry crumb mixture in a plastic bag.

By dipping the chicken pieces first in flour, second in egg-water mixture, and third in crumbs, a crisper cooked coating is achieved.

Another coating method involves rolling the chicken pieces in melted butter, then in the desired crumb mixture.

**COBBLER**—1. The name for a beverage made of wine or liquor, fruit or fruit juice, and sugar. 2. A deep-dish baked fruit dessert of American origin made with top crust only. The crust is usually made with biscuit dough rather than pastry; however, this point may be argued in some parts of the country where the pastry topping is preferred. (See also *Dessert*.)

## Fruit Cobblers

*A basic biscuit topper with fruit variations—*

> 1 cup sifted all-purpose flour
> 2 tablespoons sugar
> 1½ teaspoons baking powder
> ¼ teaspoon salt
> ¼ cup butter or margarine
> ¼ cup milk
> 1 slightly beaten egg
>   Apple, Cherry, Peach, *or*
>     Rhubarb Filling
>   Light cream *or* ice cream

For biscuit topper sift together flour, sugar, baking powder, and salt. Cut in butter or margarine till mixture resembles coarse crumbs. Combine milk and slightly beaten egg. Add all at once to dry ingredients, stirring just to moisten. Set mixture aside.

Prepare Apple, Cherry, Peach, *or* Rhubarb filling. Pour hot filling into 8¼x1¾-inch round ovenware cake dish. Immediately spoon on biscuit topper in 6 mounds. Bake at 400° for 20 to 25 minutes. Serve warm with light cream or ice cream. Makes 6 servings.

## Apple Filling

*For a treat, serve with cinnamon ice cream—*

> 1 cup sugar
> 2 tablespoons all-purpose flour
> ½ teaspoon ground cinnamon
> ¼ teaspoon ground nutmeg
> 6 cups sliced peeled apples

Combine sugar, flour, cinnamon, and nutmeg in saucepan. Toss apples with sugar mixture. Cook and stir over medium heat till apples are *almost* tender, about 7 minutes.

Crunchy pecans and tangy orange peel give the golden biscuits in Spring Rhubarb Cobbler a new dimension. Serve this dessert any season using fresh or frozen rhubarb as available.

## Cherry Filling

 1 20-ounce can pitted tart red
    cherries (water pack),
    undrained
½ cup sugar
 1 tablespoon quick-cooking
    tapioca
    Few drops red food coloring

     • • •

 1 tablespoon butter or margarine

Combine cherries, sugar, tapioca, and food coloring in saucepan. Let stand 5 minutes. Cook and stir till slightly thickened and bubbly, about 5 minutes. Stir in butter.

## Peach Filling

½ cup brown sugar
½ cup water
1½ tablespoons cornstarch
¼ teaspoon ground mace

     • • •

 4 cups sliced peaches
 1 tablespoon lemon juice
 1 tablespoon butter or margarine

Combine brown sugar, water, cornstarch, and ground mace in saucepan. Cook, stirring constantly, till mixture is thickened and bubbly. Add peaches, lemon juice, and butter. Cook till peaches are hot, about 5 minutes.

## Rhubarb Filling

　　1 cup sugar
　　2 tablespoons cornstarch
　1/4 teaspoon ground cinnamon
　　　　• • •
　　4 cups 1-inch pieces fresh rhubarb
　　1 tablespoon water
　　1 tablespoon butter or margarine

Combine sugar, cornstarch, and cinnamon in saucepan. Add rhubarb, water, and butter. Bring to boiling. Cook and stir 1 minute.

## Spring Rhubarb Cobbler

　1/3 cup sugar
　　　Dash ground cinnamon
　1 1/2 cups 1/2-inch pieces fresh rhubarb*
　1/2 cup water
　　　Few drops red food coloring
　　　　• • •
　　2 teaspoons butter or margarine
　　　Biscuit Topper

In small saucepan combine sugar and cinnamon. Add rhubarb, water, and food coloring. Cook and stir till mixture boils; cook 2 minutes more. Stir in butter or margarine. Pour rhubarb sauce into 2-cup baking dish or 2 individual casseroles. Spoon Biscuit Topper over *bubbling hot* sauce. Bake at 400° for 25 to 30 minutes. Serve with cream, if desired. Serves 2.

*Biscuit Topper:* Sift together 1/3 cup sifted all-purpose flour, 2 tablespoons sugar, 1/2 teaspoon baking powder, and dash salt. Cut in 1 1/2 tablespoons butter. Stir in 2 tablespoons milk, 2 tablespoons chopped pecans, and 1/4 teaspoon shredded orange peel. Push from spoon into two dollops atop *bubbling hot* fruit.

*For frozen rhubarb:* Thaw and drain half of a 16-ounce package frozen rhubarb, reserving syrup. Add enough water (about 2/3 cup) to syrup to make 1 cup. Blend 2 tablespoons sugar, 2 teaspoons cornstarch, and dash ground cinnamon in small saucepan; stir in rhubarb syrup and few drops red food coloring. Cook and stir till mixture bubbles. Add drained rhubarb and 2 teaspoons butter; heat through. Pour into 2-cup baking dish or 2 individual casseroles. Spoon Biscuit Topper (above) over *bubbling hot* sauce. Bake at 400° for 25 to 30 minutes. Serve with light cream, if desired. Serves 2.

## Peach-A-Berry Cobbler

　1/4 cup brown sugar
　　1 tablespoon cornstarch
　1/2 cup cold water
　　2 cups sugared sliced fresh
　　　peaches*
　　1 cup fresh blueberries*
　　1 tablespoon butter or margarine
　　1 tablespoon lemon juice
　　　　• • •
　　1 cup sifted all-purpose flour
　1/2 cup granulated sugar
　1 1/2 teaspoons baking powder
　1/2 teaspoon salt
　1/2 cup milk
　1/4 cup butter or margarine,
　　　softened
　　2 tablespoons granulated sugar
　1/4 teaspoon ground nutmeg

In saucepan mix brown sugar and cornstarch; add water. Stir in peaches and berries. Cook and stir till mixture thickens (about 3 minutes after mixture boils). Add the 1 tablespoon butter or margarine and lemon juice. Pour into 8 1/4x1 3/4-inch round ovenware cake dish.

Sift together flour, the 1/2 cup sugar, baking powder, and salt. Add milk and softened butter all at once; beat smooth. Pour over hot fruit. Mix the 2 tablespoons sugar and nutmeg. Sprinkle over batter. Bake at 350° till done, about 40 to 45 minutes. Serve warm with light cream, if desired. Makes 6 servings.

*Or use canned or frozen fruits. Drain; use 1/2 cup syrup instead of water.

## Orange Cherry Cobbler

　　1 21-ounce can cherry pie filling
　1/4 cup water
　　1 tablespoon lemon juice
　　1 package refrigerated orange
　　　Danish rolls with icing
　　　(8 rolls)

In saucepan combine pie filling, water, and lemon juice; heat to boiling. Pour into 8 1/4x1 3/4-inch round ovenware cake dish. Top *hot* cherries with rolls, cut side up. Bake at 400° until rolls are done, about 15 to 20 minutes. Spread tops with the icing that comes in the orange-roll package. Serve warm. Makes 8 servings.

572    *cock-a-leekie*

**COCK-A-LEEKIE**—A Scottish soup made with chicken broth, cut-up pieces of cooked chicken, and leeks. Sometimes prunes and raisins are added; however, the modern version contains no fruit.

**COCKLE**—A saltwater mollusk with fluted, heart-shaped shells that is harvested on seacoasts throughout the world where the cockle finds sand beds in which to live. With the shell ranging in size from about ½- to 9-inches in diameter and having a brown, yellow, or red color, they are usually sold in the United States, shelled, cooked, and canned. You'll find cockles on the gourmet shelf in grocery stores and in specialty food shops. Cockles are sweet-tasting and can be eaten raw, cooked like clams and oysters, or used in making delicious soups. (See also *Shellfish.*)

**COCKTAIL**—An alcoholic or nonalcoholic beverage, or fruit or seafood appetizer normally served before the meal.

Alcoholic cocktail beverages are mixed, iced drinks, served in glasses of all sizes. Cocktails are based on a distilled spirit, such as gin, whiskey, vodka, or rum. The exact origin of these alcoholic drinks is not known, although they are said to have originated in America during the time of Revolutionary War.

A cocktail party is a good way to entertain when space is limited. Since most of the guests remain standing, little seating space is required. Although cocktails are the main item served, appetizers and hors d'oeuvres also are offered for guests to nibble as they sip their cocktails. (If the cocktail party precedes a dinner, keep the appetizers and cocktails light.)

One of the most popular cocktails is the dry martini, a mixture of gin or vodka and dry vermouth. It can be mixed ahead of time, then chilled until serving time. Other cocktails include the Manhattan, old-fashioned, bacardi, daiquiri, or whiskey sour. If only one kind of cocktail is offered at the cocktail party, offer bourbon and/or scotch, and some nonalcoholic beverage for the abstainers.

Prepare cocktails in a shaker with ice, filling the shaker only half to two-thirds full so that the contents can be thoroughly shaken. The shaker should be large enough for a round of drinks. Two or more shakers may be used if there are a large number of guests. Cracked ice is used to chill the liquids quickly and to help mix the drink. Then, use a cocktail strainer to keep the ice in the shaker while pouring the cocktail into individual glasses.

If a shaker is not handy, cocktails can be mixed with a long-handled spoon in a pitcher. Some say that a stirred cocktail is not as diluted as a shaken cocktail.

The cocktail is often served in a glass with a stem or, if the drink is served "on the rocks" (with ice), in a short glass. It should be pleasing to the eye. That's why some cocktails are garnished with fruit or colored with fruit juices.

Nonalcoholic cocktails include fruit cups made of thoroughly chilled and attractively arranged fruit, cut in small pieces. They can be served in sherbet glasses, glass bowls, icers, or in a variety of attractive glasses. These cocktails, too, should be pleasing to the eye and may be trimmed with such colorful items as maraschino cherries or fresh mint leaves. If the fruit cocktail is the first course of a meal, do not make the servings too large.

Seafood cocktails may also be served as appetizers and may include shrimp, crab, or lobster cocktails topped off with a zippy sauce. Keep the portions small—this course is designed to stimulate the appetite, not dull it.

Nonalcoholic beverage cocktails most generally have a fruit or vegetable juice as the base. However, in recent years, undiluted canned beef bouillon, served on the rocks, has become an accepted first-course cocktail. (See *Beverages, Wines and Spirits* for additional information.)

## Summer Fruit Cocktail

In a bowl mix 2 cups sliced, peeled peaches; 1 cup diced, peeled pears; and ½ to 1 cup fresh blueberries. Combine ¼ cup lemon juice, ½ cup sugar, and dash salt, stirring to dissolve the sugar. Pour over fruits in bowl. Toss. Chill thoroughly. Spoon into stemmed sherbet glasses and garnish each serving with a fresh mint sprig. Makes 5 or 6 servings.

## 1-2-3 Fruit Cup

1 13½-ounce can pineapple
   tidbits (1⅔ cups)
1 10-ounce package frozen
   raspberries, thawed
3 tablespoons orange-flavored
   breakfast drink powder
1 11-ounce can mandarin oranges,
   drained

Drain pineapple tidbits and thawed raspberries, reserving syrups. Stir together reserved syrups and breakfast drink powder. Divide pineapple, raspberries, and oranges among 6 sherbet glasses; pour on syrup mixture. Serves 6.

## Pineapple Cocktail

2 cups unsweetened pineapple
   juice
1 cup apple juice
2 tablespoons lemon juice
1 pint pineapple sherbet
   Fresh mint

Combine pineapple, apple, and lemon juices; pour into juice glasses and chill. Just before serving, top each glass with a small scoop of pineapple sherbet and a sprig of fresh mint. Makes 6 to 8 servings.

## Tomato Zip

*A good dinner beginner—*

2¾ cups tomato juice
⅔ cup condensed beef broth
¼ cup water
1 teaspoon Worcestershire sauce
½ teaspoon onion juice
½ teaspoon prepared horseradish
   Dash pepper
3 or 4 lemon slices

In saucepan combine tomato juice, beef broth, water, Worcestershire sauce, onion juice, prepared horseradish, and pepper. Add lemon slices and heat just to boiling; remove and discard lemon slices. Serve hot. If desired, garnish each serving with an additional fresh lemon slice. Makes 4 to 6 servings.

## Shrimp Cocktail

   Cleaned, cooked shrimp
¾ cup chili sauce
2 to 4 tablespoons lemon juice
1 to 2 tablespoons prepared
   horseradish
2 teaspoons Worcestershire sauce
½ teaspoon grated onion
   Dash bottled hot pepper sauce
   Lettuce

Chill shrimp. Meanwhile, combine chili sauce, lemon juice, prepared horseradish, Worcestershire sauce, onion, and bottled hot pepper sauce. Add salt to taste. Chill thoroughly.

   Line chilled cocktail cups with lettuce. Add 4 or 5 chilled shrimp to each cocktail cup. Spoon cocktail sauce over shrimp. Serve with cocktail forks. Makes 1¼ cups sauce.

COCOA—1. A powdery food product made from cacao beans. It contains less cocoa butter than does chocolate. 2. A beverage made from the powdery substance with the addition of either milk or water.

   The processing of cocoa is the same as that used for chocolate up to the point where the nibs are made into the chocolate liquor. This liquid is processed through a hydraulic press to squeeze out part of the fat, called cocoa butter. The hard mass or cakes that remain are then crushed, ground, and sifted until they become the fine cocoa powder that is sold.

   Cocoa adds some fat to the diet in addition to minerals. One cup of cocoa beverage made with milk has 235 calories.

   How much fat cocoa adds to the diet depends on its type. Breakfast or high-fat cocoa contains at least 22 percent cocoa butter and is the type available to most consumers. Medium-fat cocoa contains 10 to 22 percent cocoa butter; whereas, low-fat cocoa contains less than 10 percent fat. These last two types are purchased predominantly for commercial use by bakers and confectioners. None of these types of cocoa have added sugar.

   There are other types of cocoa available in grocery stores. One is called Dutch-type or Dutch-process cocoa. To make this type of cocoa, an alkaline salt is added to the

Try a new use for cocoa. Make Cocoa Ripple Ring for breakfast, brunch, or afternoon treat. Either unsweetened cocoa or presweetened instant cocoa powder mix can be used.

cacao beans or chocolate liquor. This partially neutralizes the natural acids present in the cacao bean. As a result, the beverage prepared with Dutch-process cocoa will be darker in color, will have a different flavor and finer aroma, and will not settle out in the cup as readily.

Ready-to-use or instant cocoa powder mixes are also available. These mixes contain sugar, flavorings, and sometimes dried milk, in addition to the cocoa powder. Depending on the type of cocoa that is used, simply add water or milk—hot or cold—and enjoy a delightful beverage.

Store all types of cocoa in a cool, dry place in a tightly covered container to prevent the mixture from lumping.

Cocoa powder has many uses, not only as a beverage, but in baking and cooking. In baking, cocoa powder is usually blended with the dry ingredients. In a beverage, it is best to cook the cocoa with sugar and a small amount of water before adding the milk. This eliminates the raw, starchiness of the cocoa and keeps cocoa solids from settling to the bottom of the cup as quickly. Instant cocoa powder can also be used to make a delicious cake topper.

Cocoa can be substituted in a recipe calling for unsweetened chocolate if shortening is added. The substitution is 3 tablespoons unsweetened cocoa powder plus 1 tablespoon fat equals 1 ounce unsweetened chocolate. (See also *Chocolate*.)

## Breakfast Cocoa

In a saucepan mix 1/3 cup unsweetened cocoa powder, 1/3 cup sugar, and dash salt; add 1/2 cup water. Bring to boiling, stirring constantly. Boil 1 minute. Stir in 3 1/2 cups milk. Heat just to boiling point but *do not boil*. Add 1/2 teaspoon vanilla; beat with rotary beater just before serving. Float dollops of marshmallow creme atop each serving. Makes 4 cups.

## Cocoa Ripple Ring

Cream together 1/2 cup shortening, 3/4 cup sugar, and 2 eggs till light and fluffy. Sift together 1 1/2 cups sifted all-purpose flour, 2 teaspoons baking powder, and 3/4 teaspoon salt. Add to creamed mixture alternately with 2/3 cup milk, beating well after each addition. Spoon a *third* of the batter into a well-greased 6 1/2-cup mold or 9x9x2-inch baking pan.

Combine 1/3 cup instant cocoa powder mix* and 1/3 cup chopped walnuts. Sprinkle *half* of the cocoa mixture over batter in pan. Repeat layers, ending with batter. Bake at 350° for 35 minutes. Let stand 5 minutes. Turn out of mold. Serve warm. Makes 12 servings.

*Or, substitute 1/4 cup sugar and 2 tablespoons unsweetened cocoa powder for the mix.

## Cocoa Fudge Cake

> 3/4 cup butter or margarine
> 1 1/2 cups sugar
> 3 eggs
> 1 1/2 teaspoons vanilla
> 1 teaspoon red food coloring
> 2 1/4 cups sifted cake flour
> 1/2 cup unsweetened cocoa powder
> 3 teaspoons baking powder

Cream butter and sugar till light. Separate eggs. Add yolks, one at a time, beating well after each. Add vanilla and food coloring. Sift together dry ingredients. Add to creamed mixture alternately with 1 cup cold water, beating after each addition.

Beat egg whites till soft peaks form. Fold into batter. Bake in 2 greased and floured 9x 1 1/2-inch round cake pans at 350° till done, about 25 minutes. Cool 10 minutes before removing from pans. Cool completely; frost.

## Chocolate Daisy Cupcakes

> 1/2 cup butter or margarine
> 1 1/2 cups sugar
> 2 eggs
> 2 cups sifted all-purpose flour
> 1/4 cup unsweetened cocoa powder
> 1 teaspoon baking soda
> 1/2 teaspoon salt
>
> • • •
>
> 2 teaspoons instant tea powder
> 1 cup cold water
> 1 teaspoon vanilla
> 1 can ready-to-spread chocolate
>     frosting
> **Whole blanched almonds**

Cream butter and sugar together till light and fluffy. Add eggs, one at a time, beating well after each. Sift together flour, cocoa powder, baking soda, and salt.

Dissolve tea in the cold water; add vanilla. Alternately add dry ingredients and tea mixture to creamed mixture, beating well after each addition. Line muffin pans with paper bake cups. Fill each half-full. Bake at 350° about 20 minutes. Cool completely. Frost with the chocolate frosting. Arrange whole nuts on each to make a "daisy." Makes 2 dozen cupcakes.

Cocoa powders include Dutch-process cocoa (left), unsweetened cocoa (center), and instant ready-to-use cocoa mix (right).

Dress-up wedges of fluffy angel cake with easy Minted Cocoa Fluff. Pass crushed peppermint candy for a colorful topper.

## Cocoa-Mint Wafers

    1 tablespoon vinegar
  ¼ cup milk
  ½ cup shortening
    1 cup sugar
    1 egg
  ¼ to ½ teaspoon peppermint
       extract
    2 cups sifted all-purpose flour
  ½ cup unsweetened cocoa powder
  ½ teaspoon baking soda

Add vinegar to milk; set aside. Cream together shortening and sugar. Add egg, extract, and milk. Sift together remaining ingredients and ¼

teaspoon salt. Add to creamed mixture, blending well. Shape in rolls about 2 inches in diameter. Wrap in waxed paper; chill 4 to 6 hours.

Slice rolls into thin cookies and place on *ungreased* cookie sheet. Bake at 350° for 6 to 8 minutes. Makes about 6 dozen cookies.

## Minted Cocoa Fluff

Combine 1 cup whipping cream, ½ cup instant cocoa powder mix, and 1 or 2 drops peppermint extract; chill. Whip till stiff.

Serve on slices of angel food cake; top each serving with crushed peppermint stick candy. Makes 1½ cups topping.

## Peanut Butter-Oatmeal Bars

  ½ cup shortening
  ½ cup granulated sugar
  ½ cup brown sugar
  ⅓ cup peanut butter
  ½ teaspoon vanilla
    1 egg
  ¼ cup milk

    1 cup sifted all-purpose flour
  ½ teaspoon baking soda
    1 cup quick-cooking rolled oats
    2 cups sifted confectioners'
       sugar
  ¼ cup unsweetened cocoa powder
    3 tablespoons butter, melted
  ½ teaspoon vanilla
    Icing

Cream together first 5 ingredients till fluffy. Add egg and milk; beat well. Sift together flour, baking soda, and ½ teaspoon salt. Add to creamed mixture. Beat just till combined. Stir in rolled oats. Spread mixture evenly in greased 13x9x2-inch baking pan. Bake at 350° for 20 minutes. Cool thoroughly.

Sift together confectioners' sugar and cocoa. Quickly stir in melted butter, 2 to 3 tablespoons boiling water, and ½ teaspoon vanilla. Beat till smooth. Spread quickly and evenly over cooled cookies in pan.

*Icing:* Heat and stir 2 tablespoons butter or margarine till golden brown. Stir in 1 cup sifted confectioners' sugar and 3 to 4 teaspoons milk. Drizzle over cookies. Cut in bars.